Code Of Canon Law

Canon 66 "The Christian economy, therefore, since it is the new and definitive Covenant, will never pass away; and no new public revelation is to be expected before the glorious manifestation of our Lord Jesus Christ." Yet even if Revelation is already complete, it has not been made completely explicit; it remains for Christian faith gradually to grasp its full significance over the course of the centuries.

Canon 67 Throughout the ages, there have been so-called "private" revelations, some of which have been recognized by the authority of the Church. They do not belong, however, to the deposit of faith. It is not their role to improve or complete Christ's definitive Revelation, but to help live more fully by it in a certain period of history. Guided by the Magisterium of the Church, the sensus fidelium knows how to discern and welcome in these revelations whatever constitutes an authentic call of Christ or his saints to the Church.

Christian faith cannot accept "revelations" that claim to surpass or correct the Revelation of which Christ is the fulfilment, as is the case in certain non-Christian religions and also in certain recent sects which base themselves on such "revelations."

The Full of Grace:
The Early Years.
The Merit.
Joseph's Passion.
The Blue Angel.
The Boyhood of Jesus.

Follow Me:
Treasure with 7 Names
Where there are Thorns, there also will be roses
For Love that Perseveres
The Apostolic College
The Decalogue

The Chronicles of Jesus & Judas Iscariot:
I See You As You Are
Those who are Marked
Jesus Weeps

Lazarus:
That Beautiful Blonde
Flowers of Bounty

Claudia Procula:
Do You Love the Nazarene?
The Caprice of Court Morals

Christian Tenets:
On Reincarnation

Mary of Magdala:
Ah! My Beloved! I Reached You At Last!

Lamb Books
Illustrated adaptations for the whole family

LAMB BOOKS

Published by Lamb Books, 2 Dalkeith Court, 45 Vincent Street, London SW1P 4HH;

UK, USA, FR, IT, SP, PT, DE

www.lambbooks.org

First published by Lamb Books 2013
This edition
001

The author and publisher are grateful to the Centro Editoriale Valtoriano in Italy for
Permission to quote from the Poem of the Man- God by Maria Valtorta, by Valtorta
Publishing

Set in Bookman Old Style R
Printed and bound by CPI Group (UK) Ltd, Croydon, CR0, 4YY

Follow Me

Treasure With 7 Names

LAMBBOOKS

Acknowledgements

The material in this book is adapted from The Mystical City of God, by Sister Mary of Jesus of Agreda, which received the Imprimatur in 1949 and also from The Poem of the Man God (The Gospel As Revealed To Me), first approved by Pope Pius XII in 1948, when in a meeting on February 26th 1948, witnessed by three other priests, he ordered the three priest present to "Publish this work as it is". In 1994, the Vatican heeded to the calls of Christians worldwide and have begun to examine the case for the Canonization of Maria Valtorta (Little John).

The Poem of the Man God was described by Pope Pius' confessor as "edifying". Mystical revelations have long been the province of priests and the religious. Now, they are accessible to all. May all who read this adaptation also find it edifying. And through this light, may Faith be renewed.

Special Thanks to the Centro Editoriale Valtortiano in Italy for permission to quote from the Poem of the Man God by Maria Valtorta, nick named, Little John.

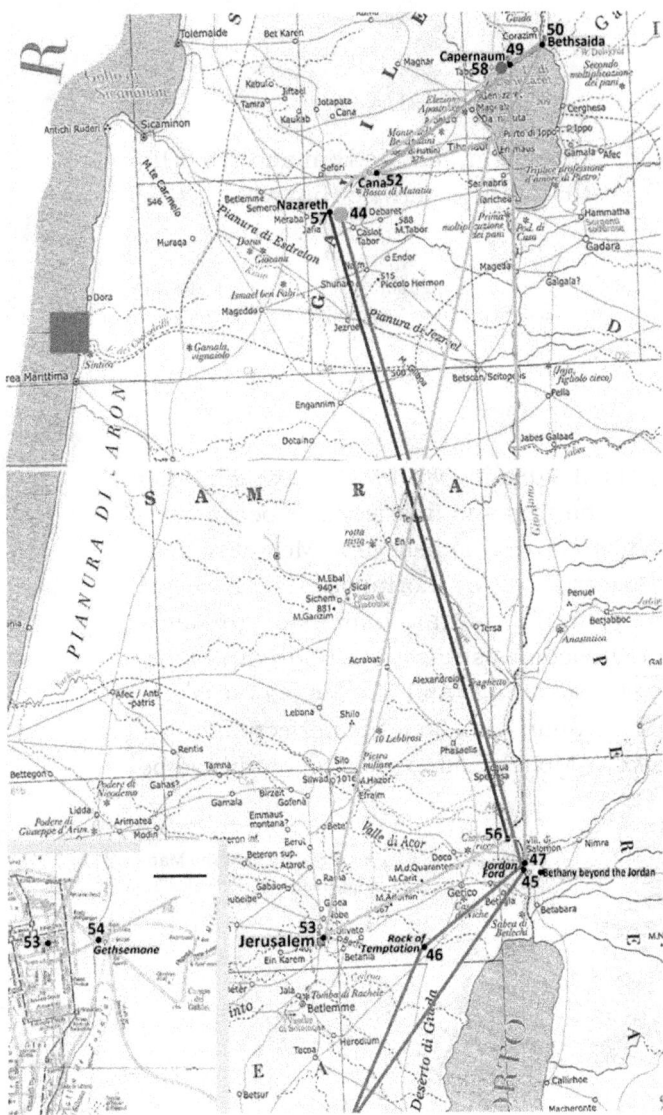

"Receive thy Onlybegotten Son, imitate Him and rear Him; and remember, that thou must sacrifice Him when I shall demand it of Thee"

The Holy Trinity to the Virgin Mary at the cave of the Nativity
.-Mystical City of God by Venerable Mary of Jesus of Agreda

"... With so many books dealing with Me and which, after so many revisions, changes and fineries have become unreal, I want to give those who believe in Me a vision brought back to the truth of My mortal days. I am not diminished thereby, on the contrary I am made greater in My humility, which becomes substantial nourishment for you, to teach you to be humble and like Me, as I was a man like you and in My human life I bore the perfection of a God. I was to be your Model, and models must always be perfect."

Jesus, February 9th 1944-Poem of the Man-God
(The Gospel As Revealed To Me)

The Death Of Joseph

Extract from 'The Mystical City of God'
By Venerable Mary of Jesus of Agreda.

For the past eight years, Joseph has been infirmed and suffering with arthritis during which time his soul has been purified in the fire of divine love. As time passed, his strength diminished and the care given him by his Spouse increased measure for measure. When Mary, in Her exalted wisdom perceives that the end is near, She petitions Her Son on Joseph's behalf:

"Lord God Most High, Son of the eternal Father and Saviour of the world, by Your divine light I see the hour approaching which You have decreed for the death of Your servant Joseph. I beseech You, by Your ancient mercies and infinite bounty, to assist him in that hour by Your almighty power. Let his death be as precious in Your eyes, as the uprightness of his life was pleasing to You, so that he may depart in peace and in the hope of the eternal reward to be given to him on the day in

which You shall open the gates of heaven for all the faithful. Be mindful, my Son, of the humility and love of Your servant; of his exceeding great merits and virtues; of the fidelity, care and concern by which this just man has supported You and me, Your humble handmaid, in the sweat of his brow."

"My Mother, Your request is pleasing to me, and the merits of Joseph are acceptable in my eyes. I will now assist him and will assign him a place among the princes of my people so high that he will be the admiration of the angels and will cause them and all men to break forth in highest praise. With none of the human born shall I do as with Your spouse."

Mary thanks Her Son for this promise.

For nine days and nights before his death, Joseph enjoys the uninterrupted company and attendance of Mary or of Jesus. Three times on each of the nine days, the angels entertain Joseph with heavenly music, mixing hymns of praise with blessings. During this time, their home is scented with sweet fragrance so wonderful that it comforts Joseph and invigorates all who come near the house.

So that his death might be more the triumph of his love than of the effects of original sin, Jesus suspends the miraculous support that had enabled Joseph to withstand the force of his love during his life time thus enabling his soul to break the bonds that held it within its mortal body. Thus, the real cause of Joseph's death is excessive love.

A day before his passing, Joseph slips into an ecstasy that lasts twenty four hours, in which he sees the divine Essence clearly and also sees all that he had believed by faith including the mysteries of the Incarnation and Redemption and the Church with its Sacraments. Then he is commissioned and assigned as the messenger of Christ to the holy Patriarchs in Limbo, to prepare them for their release into Paradise.

All this, Mary sees reflected in the soul of Her Son and She offers Her sincerest thanks to the Almighty.

When Joseph recovers from the ecstasy, his face shines with wonderful splendour reflecting his soul now transformed by his vision of the essence of God. He asks Mary for Her blessing but She goes to Her divine Son that He might bless him in Her stead.

Now, at the age of sixty, having been the spouse of Mary the Mother of the Word Incarnate for twenty seven years, the moment of the death of Joseph has arrived when Mary is forty one and a half- though She never looks older than thirty three- and Jesus, twenty six and a half.

End of Extract.

Jesus is at work in the carpenter's workshop where the southern and eastern walls are built of plastered rock carved out of natural grottos in the rocky mountain, which also constitutes its northern and western walls.

A little pot of glue sits on a rustic wood fireplace in the recess of the rock, so blackened with smoke over many years that it looks though it is covered with tar. There is a hole in the wall, covered with a large tile and serves as a chimney for letting out the smoke but it must function very poorly because the other walls are also blackened with smoke and even now, the little workshop is filled with a smoky mist.

Jesus, now a grown man, is working at a large carpentry bench, planing boards which He then rests against the wall behind Him. He frees a stool clamped on two sides with a vice and carefully examines it from every angle, checking to see that it is perfect. Then he goes to the fireplace, takes the little pot and stirs its contents with a little brush that ends as a little stick.

His tunic is rather short, dark hazelnut in colour, with the sleeves rolled up to His elbows. He has a workman's apron over his tunic, which He uses to wipe His fingers after touching the pot.

He is alone, working diligently but peacefully, His movements smooth and patient as He planes a resistant knot on the wood. A screwdriver falls down from the work-bench twice and He picks it up patiently. And He does not mind the smoke in the little room that must irritate His eyes.

Now and again, He raises His head and looks at the closed door in the southern wall that leads into the little room that looks out into the kitchen garden; He looks and He listens.
Once, He opens the door in the eastern wall that looks out unto the dusty road and He looks out as one expecting another then goes back to His work, not sad but very serious.

He is working on a part of a wheel when Mary comes in through the southern door, bar headed and wearing a simple dark blue tunic tied at the waist with a cord of the same colour. She rushes to Jesus, worry written on Her face of a blue angel, tears shining in Her reddened and tired eyes and placing both Her hands on His arm in an attitude of prayer and sorrow, She says with trembling lips:
'Oh! Jesus! Come, come. He is very ill!'

'Mother!' He answers simply and in the one word, speaks volumes, whilst He passes His arm over Her shoulder, caresses and comforts Her.
Then leaving His work, He takes of His apron and

goes out with Her through the southern door and into the adjoining room filled with light streaming in from the kitchen garden that is also full of light and green, and where there are doves fluttering around the clothes hung out to dry in the blowing wind.

The room is poor but tidy. On a low bed covered with small mattresses, lies Joseph, leaning on cushions. The livid paleness of his face, the lifelessness of his eyes, his panting chest and the total relaxation of his body all say he is dying.

Standing by Joseph's left hand side, Mary takes his hand, now wrinkled near its nails and rubs, caresses and kisses it. Then, with a small piece of cloth, She dries the lines of perspiration glistening on his temples and wipes away a glassy tear in the corner of his eye. Then She dips another piece of linen into a liquid that looks like wine and moistens his lips with it.

From Joseph's right hand side, Jesus quickly and carefully lifts Joseph's slumping body back unto the cushions, adjusting them with Mary's help. Then He caresses the forehead of the dying man and tries to encourage him.

Large tears, like bright sapphires roll silently down Mary's pale cheeks and unto Her dark blue dress as She weeps silently.

Recovering somewhat, Joseph looks up at Jesus, takes His hand like he wants to say something and to receive strength for this last trial from his divine Son. Jesus bends over the hand and kisses it, making Joseph smile.

Then turning round and searching with his eyes, Joseph looks for Mary and also smiles at Her. Mary tries to smile back at Joseph from Her kneeling position by his bedside, does not succeed and instead bows Her head. Joseph lays his hand on Her bowed head with a chaste caress that looks like a blessing.

All around them is silent except for the fluttering and cooing of the doves, the rustling of the leaves and the warbling of the water outside... and the breathing of the dying man in the room.

Jesus goes round the bed, takes a stool and makes Mary sit on it, once again simply saying 'Mother!'

Then He goes back to His place, takes Joseph's hand in His and bending over the dying man, He whispers this psalm to him:

Look after me, o Lord, because I hoped in You...

In favour of his friends who live on his earth

he has accomplished all my wishes in a wonderful way...

I will bless the Lord Who is my advisor...

The Lord is always before me.

He is on my right-hand side that I may not fall.

Therefore my heart exults and my tongue rejoices

and also my body will rest in hope.

Because You will not abandon my soul

in the dwelling place of the dead,

neither will You allow Your friend to see corruption.

You will reveal the path of light to me

and will fill me with joy showing me Your face."

Cheering up a little, Joseph looks at his foster Son, gives Him a lively smile and presses His fingers. Jesus answers with a smile of His own and a caress. And still bending over His foster father, He goes on softly:

How I love your Tabernacles, o Lord.

My soul yearns and pines for the courts of the Lord.

Also the sparrow has found a home

and the little dove a nest for its young.

I am longing for your Altars, Lord.

Happy those who live in Your house...

happy the man who finds his strength in You.

He inspired into his heart the ascents

from the valley of tears to the chosen place.

O Lord hear my prayer...

O God, turn Your eyes and look at the face of Your Anointed..."

Joseph sobs, looks at Jesus and makes an effort to speak as if to bless Him but he cannot. It is clear that he understands but is unable to speak. But he is happy and looks at his Jesus with liveliness and trust. Jesus goes on:

Oh! Lord, You have favoured Your own country,

You brought back the captives of Jacob...

Show us, o Lord, Your mercy and bring us back Your Saviour.

I want to listen to what the Lord is saying to me.

He will certainly speak of peace to His people,

for His friends and for those who convert their hearts to Him.

Yes, His saving help is near...

and the glory will live in our country.

Love and loyalty have now met,

righteousness and peace have now embraced.

Loyalty reaches up from the earth

and righteousness leans down from Heaven.

Yes, the Lord Himself bestows happiness and our soil gives its harvest.

Righteousness will always precede Him and will leave its footprints on the path."

'You have seen that hour, father, and you have worked for it...' Says Jesus '... You have cooperated in the formation of this hour and the Lord will reward you for it. I am telling you.' And Jesus wipes away a

tear of joy running slowing down Joseph's cheek.
Then He resumes:

"O Lord, remember David and all his kindness.

How he swore to the Lord: I will not enter my house,

*nor climb into the bed of my rest, nor allow my eyes to
sleep,*

nor give rest to my eyelids, nor peace to my temples

*until I have found a place for the Lord, a home for the
God of Jacob...*

Rise, o Lord and come to Your resting place,

You and Your Ark of holiness..."

Mary understands and bursts into tears.

*May Your priests vest in virtue and Your devout shout
for joy.*

For the sake of Your servant David,

do not deprive us of the face of Your Anointed.

The Lord swore to David and will remain true to His word:

'I will put on your throne the fruit of your womb'.

The Lord has chosen His home...

I will make a horn sprout for David,

I will trim a lamp for My Anointed."

'Thank you my father on My behalf and on behalf of My Mother. You have been a Just father to Me and the Eternal Father chose you as the guardian of His Christ and of His Ark. You have been the lamp trimmed for Him and for the fruit of the holy womb, you have had a loving heart. Go in peace, father. Your Widow will not be helpless. God has arranged that She must not be alone. Go peacefully to your rest, I tell you' says Jesus.

Mary is weeping with Her face buried in the mantles that serve as blankets, stretched over Joseph's body, now growing cold. He is now breathing with difficulty and Jesus hastens to comfort him as his eyes grow dim once again.

Happy the man who fears the Lord

and joyfully keeps His commandments...

His righteousness will last forever.

For the upright He shines like a lamp in the dark,

He is merciful, tender-hearted, virtuous...

The just man will be remembered forever.

His justice is eternal and his power will rise and become a glory..."

'You, father, will have that glory. I will soon come and take you, with the Patriarchs who have gone before you, to the glory, which awaits you. May your spirit rejoice in My word.'

"Who lives in the shelter of the Most High,

lives under the protection of the God of Heaven."

You live there, o father.

*'He rescued me from the snares of fowlers and from
rough words.*

He will cover you with His wings

and under His feathers you will find shelter.

His truth will protect you like a shield

and you need not fear the terrors of night...

No evil will come near you because

He ordered His angels to guard you wherever you go.

They will support you on their hands

so that you may not hurt your foot against stones.

You will tread on lions and adders,

you will trample on savage lions and dragons.

Because you have hoped in the Lord,

*He says to you, o father, that He will free you and
protect you.*

Because you have lifted your voice to Him, He will hear you,

He will be with you in your last affliction,

He will glorify you after this life,

showing you even now His Salvation."

'And in the future life, He will let you enter, because of the Saviour Who is now comforting you and Who, very soon, oh! I repeat it, He will come very soon and hold you in His divine embrace and take you, at the head of all the Patriarchs, where the dwelling place has been prepared for the Just man of God who was My blessed father.'

As Joseph sinks into the mists of death, Jesus raises His voice to reach Joseph's heart, whose end is impending, his breathing now painful and panting whilst Mary caresses him.

'Go before Me and tell the Patriarchs that the Saviour is in the world and the Kingdom of Heaven will soon be opened to them. Go, father, may My blessing accompany you.'

Sitting on the edge of the little bed, Jesus embraces and draws to Himself, the dying man, who collapses and passes away peacefully.

There is solemn peace in the little room. Jesus lays the Patriarch down again and embraces Mary, Who at the last moment, broken hearted, had come near Jesus.

Extract from 'The Mystical City of God'
By Venerable Mary of Jesus of Agreda.

Mary suffers bitterly for the loss of the spouse whom She loved deeply, to whom She had devoted twenty-seven years of faithful life and who, for Her, had been a father, a spouse, a brother, a friend and a protector.

Now, lonely as the shoot of a vine when the tree to which it is tied is cut down, it is as though Her house has been struck by thunder and splitting. Once a unit in which the members supported one another, now, its main wall is missing, a first blow to the Family and a sign of the impending departure of Her Beloved.

Once more, the will of the eternal Father imposes upon Her widowhood, demanding separation from Her Creature. And in the same little house in Nazareth where twenty seven years before She had become spouse and Mother, in tears, She gives the same sublime answer:

'Yes. Yes, Lord, let it be done to Me according to Your word.'

For the strength to give that answer, Mary had drawn near to Jesus in the last moments of Joseph's life, so that She might always be united to God in the gravest hours of Her life: as She was in the Temple, when She was asked to marry Joseph, at Nazareth when She was called to Maternity, now again at Nazareth shedding the tears of a widow, and in a short while, once again at Nazareth in the dreadful separation of Her Son, as She will be on Calvary, helplessly watching Him tortured and then seeing Him die.

Farewell To His Mother And Departure From Nazareth

Extract from 'The Mystical City of God'
By Venerable Mary of Jesus of Agreda.

As it is impossible for man or angels to measure Mary's love for Her Son, we resort to Her actions as well as Her joys and Her sorrows as a standard by which we measure this love.

For She loves Jesus as the Son of the eternal Father equal to Him in essence and in all divine attributes and perfections. She loves Him as Her natural Son in so far as He is man formed of Her own flesh and blood. She loves Him because as man, He is the saint of all Saints and the cause of all holiness. She loves Him because He is the most beautiful among the sons of men, the most dutiful Son of His Mother and Her most magnificent Champion since it is His son-ship that has raised Her to the highest dignity possible amongst creatures, and elevated Her above all with the treasures of His Divinity, decorated Her with dominion over all creation together with favours, blessings and graces as never before or since conferred upon another being.

She fully understands and is grateful for all these motives of Her love, together with many others that only Her superior love can appreciate. In Her heart, there is no obstacle or limitation to love since it is most innocent and pure; She is grateful because Her profound humility urges Her to a most faithful conformity, She is not careless since She is full of grace and enthusiasm to serve conscientiously. Neither is She forgetful since Her faithful memory is constantly fixed upon the blessings received and the reasons and the doctrine of deepest love. She moves in the sphere of divine love itself since She lives in His visible presence, attends the school of divine love of Her Son, copying Him in everything in His very company.

Nothing is wanting to this peerless One among lovers for entertaining love without limitation in measure or manner; this most beautiful Moon, now at its fullness and looking into this Sun of justice that has risen like a divine aurora from height to height and is now at its noon splendour with the most clear light of grace. This Moon, Mary, detached from all material creatures and entirely transformed by the light of this Sun, having experienced on Her part, all the effects of His reciprocal love, favours and gifts. In this height of

Her blessedness, at a time when the loss of all these blessings in Her Son makes it most painful,
She hears the voice of the eternal Father calling, as once He called upon Abraham, and demanding Her beloved Isaac, the deposit of all Her love and hope.

Mary was not unaware that the time of Her sacrifice was near since Jesus has already turned thirty and the time and place for satisfying the debt He has assumed is at hand. But in the full possession of the Treasure, which is all Her happiness, Mary still considers its loss as far off. Notwithstanding, the hour is now upon Her and She becomes enveloped in a vision, is placed in the presence of the throne of the Holy Trinity and from it issues a voice of wonderful power saying:

"Mary, My Daughter and Spouse, offer to Me your Onlybegotten Son in sacrifice."

By the living power of these words, She receives light, intelligence and understanding of the will of the Almighty and of the decree of the Redemption of man through the Passion and Death of Her Son, together with all that will happen from now on in His preaching and his public life. As this knowledge is renewed and perfected in Her, She feels Her soul overpowered by sentiments of subjection, humility, love of God and man, compassion and tender sorrow for all that Her Son will suffer.

But with a steadfast and charitable heart, She gives answer to the Almighty:

"Eternal King and omnipotent God of infinite wisdom and goodness, all that has being outside of You exists solely for Your mercy and greatness, and You are undiminished Lord of all. How then do You command me, an insignificant wormlet of the earth, to sacrifice and deliver over to Your will the Son, whom Your condescension has given me?...

He is Yours, eternal Father, since from all eternity before the morning star You gave rise to Him and You have Him and shall have Him through all the eternities and if I have clothed Him in the form of servant in my womb and from my own blood, and if I have nourished his humanity at my breast and ministered to it as a Mother: this most holy humanity is also Your property, and so am I, since I have received from You all that I am and that I could give Him...

What then can I offer to You, that is not more Yours than mine?...
I confess, most high King, that Your magnificence and beneficence are so liberal in heaping upon Your creatures Your infinite treasures, that in order to bind Yourself to them You wish to receive from them as a free gift, even Your own Onlybegotten Son, Him whom You brought into being from Your own substance *and from the light of Your Divinity. With Him came to me all blessings together and from his hands I received immense gifts and graces; He is the Virtue of my virtue,*

31

the Substance of my spirit, Life of my soul and Soul of my life, the Sustenance of all my joy of living. It would be a sweet sacrifice, indeed, to yield Him up to You who alone knows his value; but to yield Him for the satisfaction of Your justice into the hands of his cruel enemies at the cost of his life, more precious than all the works of creation; this indeed, most high Lord, is a great sacrifice which You ask of his Mother...

However let not my will but thine be done. Let the freedom of the human race be thus bought; let Your justice and equity be satisfied; let Your infinite love become manifest; let Your name be known and magnified before all creatures...
I deliver Him over into Your hands before all creatures. I deliver over into Your hands my beloved Isaac, that He may be truly sacrificed; ...
I offer my Son, the Fruit of my womb, in order that, according to the unchangeable decree of Your Will, He may pay the debt contracted not by his fault, but by the children of Adam, and in order that in his Death He may fulfil all that Your holy Prophets, inspired by You, have written and foretold."

This, the greatest and most acceptable sacrifice that ever has been or ever will be made to the eternal Father from the beginning of creation to its end, outside of that to be made by His own Son, the Redeemer; and is most intimately connected with, and like to that which He will offer.

If the greatest charity is to offer one's life for the beloved, then without doubt, Mary's charity far exceeds this highest degree of love towards men because She loves Her Son much more than Her own life. As Christ said to Nicodemus (John 15,7): So God loved the world that He gave His only Son in order that none of those who believed in Him might perish, so it is in proportion with Mary, Mother of mercy, Who loves mankind so much that She gives Her only Son for its salvation. And had Her sacrifice not been given in this manner when it was asked of Her, the salvation of men would not have been executed since this decree was to be fulfilled on the condition that the Mother's will coincided with that of the eternal Father. Such is the obligation that the children of Adam owe to Mary.

Having accepted the sacrifice of Mary, God comforts Her with the life giving bread of heavenly understanding so that with invincible fortitude, She might assist the Incarnate Word in the work of the Redemption as Co-Redeemer. Therefore, still in the same vision, Mary is raised into a more exalted ecstasy in which by the clear light of the essence of God, She understands God's desire to communicate His treasures to mankind through the works of the Incarnate Word and sees the glories that these works will bring to the name of God. This knowledge fills Her soul with so much jubilation that She renews Her offering of Her divine Son to the Father

When She recovers from this vision, by its effects and the strength received through it, She is now prepared to separate from Her divine Son, Who, for His part, has already resolved upon his baptism and His fast in the desert.

He calls His mother and speaks to Her with love and compassion saying:

"My Mother, my existence as man I derive entirely from Your substance and blood, of which I have taken the form of a servant in Your virginal womb. You also have nursed Me at Your breast and taken care of Me by Your labours and sweat. For this reason I account Myself more Your Son than any other ever acknowledged or ever will acknowledge himself as the son of his mother. Give Me Your permission and consent toward accomplishing the will of my eternal Father. Already the time has arrived, in which I must leave Your sweet interaction and company and begin the work of the Redemption of man. The time of rest has come to an end and the hour of suffering for the rescue of the sons of Adam has arrived. But I wish to perform this work of my Father with Your assistance, and You are to be my companion and helper in preparing for my Passion and Death on the Cross. Although I must now leave You alone, my blessing and my loving and powerful protection will remain with You. Afterwards, I will

return to claim Your assistance and company in my
labours; for I am to undergo them in the form of man,
which You have given Me."

With these words, Jesus places his arms around His
Mothers neck and they comfort each other whilst
Mother and Son overflow with abundant tears.

Then Mary falls at His feet and answers:
"My Lord and eternal God: You are indeed my Son and
in You is fulfilled all the force of love, which I have
received of You: my inmost soul is laid open to the eyes
of Your divine wisdom. My life I would account but
little, if I could thereby save Your own, or if I could die
for You many times. But the will of the eternal Father
and Your own must be fulfilled and I offer my own will
as a sacrifice for this fulfilment. Receive it, my Son and
as Master of all my being; let it be an acceptable
offering, and let Your divine protection never be
wanting to me. It would be a much greater sacrifice for
me, to be allowed to accompany You in Your labours
and in Your Cross. May I merit this favour, my Son, and
I ask it of You as Your true Mother in return for the
human form, which You have received of me."

Having asked to partake in the sufferings and labours
of Christ, Her request is granted and from the time
Christ begins His Mission, She will be deprived of the
tokens of tenderness which until now have been

customary between Mother and Son and which have been Her delight. He begins to treat Mary with greater reserve, even addressing Her as 'Woman' instead of 'Mother' as He will do at the wedding in Cana and also on Golgotha, as an exquisite refinement of His affection in order to assimilate Her into His sufferings.

The matter thus settled, Mother and Son prepare to separate.

End of Extract.

It is His last meal at home before His mission begins. Served in the front room at Nazareth, that also doubles as the room where the family take their rest. In the room is a plain rectangular table, on the other side of which is a chest that also serves as a seat, set against the wall. Also in the room are Mary's loom and a stool set against one wall, and two more stools and a book case that also holds oil lamps and other objects.

Through the open door that leads into the kitchen garden, the faint evening sun rays light the upper foliage of a tree beginning to turn green with its first leaves.

Jesus is seated at the table, at super served by Mary who comes and goes from the kitchen. From His seat, He can see the light of the fireplace through the open door. On the table, there is already some flat dark brown bread, an amphora with water and a goblet on the table. Mary serves some boiled vegetables and then later, some roasted fish and finally, some soft fresh cheese like rounded pebbles served with some small dark olives. Twice or three times, Jesus asks Mary to sit down and eat with Him but each time She shakes Her head, smiling sadly.

Silently, He eats, looking at His mother sadly, Who, also visibly sad, comes and goes purely to occupy Herself. Though it is still daylight, She lights a lamp and sets it on the table near Jesus, subtly caressing His head as She does so. Then, opening a nut-brown knapsack made of pure waterproof wool, She looks inside it, goes back into the storeroom at the far end of the kitchen and returns with some withered apples preserved from last summer and puts them in the knapsack, adding a loaf of bread and some cheese although Jesus remarks that He does not want them as there is already enough food in His satchel.

Then She comes to the shorter end of the table and standing by His left hand side, She watches Him with love and adoration as He eats, Her face paler than usual; momentarily aged by pain, Her tired, ringed, sorrowful eyes bigger and brighter from tears already shed and tears welling up within.

Jesus, more pensive than usual, is eating slowly, not from hunger but to please His Mother. And now, lifting up His head, He looks at His Mother, their eyes meet and seeing that Hers are full of tears, He bows His head again so She might be free to weep. But He takes Her slender hand that is resting on the table, in His left hand, lifts it to His cheek and rubs His cheek and then His face on it to feel the caress of the poor trembling hand, and kisses it on the back with love and respect.

Mary stifles a sob with Her left hand and wipes away the tears streaming down Her face with Her fingers.

Jesus resumes His meal and Mary goes out into the kitchen garden now shrouded in twilight. Jesus stops eating and resting His left elbow on the table, leans His forehead in His hand, absorbed in thought.

Then He listens, gets up from the table and follows Mary outside. He looks about then moves right and enters, the carpenter's workshop now tidied; no boards or shavings lying around, the fire out and the tools laid aside.

Bending over the large work-bench, Her head resting on Her folded left arm, Mary is weeping silently but grievously. Jesus approaches Her so softly, She does not realise He's there until He lays His hand on Her lowered head.
'Mother!' He says simply and in His voice, there is a gentle loving reproach.

Mary raises Her head and looks at Jesus through a

veil of tears. And then She leans on His right arm
with both hands joined as though in prayer. Jesus
wipes Her face with the hem of His large sleeve and
then embraces Her, clasping Her to His heart and
kissing Her forehead, majestic and manly whilst
Mary, but for Her sorrow stricken face, looks like a
little girl.

'Come Mother' says Jesus to Her and holding Her
close with His right arm, they go back outside into the
kitchen garden and sit down together on a bench set
against the wall of the house. The garden is now
silent and dark, lit only by the moonlight and the
light coming from the house. The night is serene.
Jesus talks to Mary quietly- a mere whisper, and
Mary listens and nods in assent:

'...And get Your relatives to come. Don't stay here
alone. I will be happier, Mother, and You know how I
need peace of mind to fulfil My mission...You will not
lack My love. I will come quite often and I will inform
You, in case I cannot come home, when I am back in
Galilee. Then You will come to Me, Mother...This hour
was to come. It began when the angel appeared to
You; the hour strikes now and we must live it,
Mother, must we not?....

...After we have overcome the trial, we shall have
peace and joy. First, we must cross this desert as did
our Ancestors before they entered the Promised Land.
And the Lord God will help us as He helped them...He

will grant us His help as a spiritual manna to nourish our souls in the difficult moment of the trial...Let us say the Our Father together...'

They stand up and look up to Heaven: two living victims shining in the darkness. With Mary's hands joined, and His hands outstretched in the fashion of a priest, Slowly, in a clear voice, Jesus says the Lord's prayer, emphasising "Thy Kingdom come" and then after a pause, also emphasising "Thy will be done".

They return to the house.

Jesus pours some wine from an amphora on the bookcase into a goblet and sets the goblet on the table. Then He takes Mary's hand and makes Her sit by His side and drink some wine, into which He dips a small slice of bread and, after some resistance, makes Her eat it. Jesus drains the goblet. Then clasping His Mother to His side, He holds Her close to His heart and they sit thus for a while, silent...waiting. Mary caresses Jesus' right hand and His knees and Jesus pats Mary's arm and Her head.

After some time, Jesus rises and so does Mary. They embrace and kiss each other fondly time and time again. Every time they seem about to separate, Mary embraces Her Creature over and over again; the suffering Mother, Who must part with Her Son, fully knowing what lies ahead.

Jesus puts His dark blue mantle over His shoulders, pulls on the hood and carries His knapsack on His back in order to walk with His hands free. Mary helps Him and takes Her time sorting out His tunic, mantle and hood, delaying the inevitable.

Jesus makes a sign of blessing in the room and then goes towards the door. At the open door they kiss once again. Then Jesus departs into the night and onto the silent road, a solitary figure walking away in the white moonlight.

With his first steps outside the house, Jesus raises His eyes to Heaven and offers with infinite love to the Father, all that he is about to undertake for the salvation of mankind: his labours, sorrows, passion and death on the cross and the natural grief of parting as a true and loving Son from His Mother Who's sweet company He has enjoyed for thirty years.

Mary, leaning against the door post, paler than the moon's rays, eyes sparkling with silent tears, watches Him go farther and farther away along the narrow white road. Twice, He turns round to look at His Mother still leaning, weeping against the doorpost, watching Him depart through Her veil of tears. Then Jesus disappears round a bend ...the start of His Evangelical journey, which will end on Golgotha...

Mary goes back into the house, still in tears, and
closes the door...She has also begun Her journey,

which will take Her to Golgotha...

...For mankind, who remains ungrateful to those Two Who have climbed Calvary for them.

Jesus sets out to seek the Baptist to be baptised on the banks of the Jordan. Before He arrives at the Jordan, He fills the Baptist with new light and joy giving him a clearer vision of the hypostatic union of the person of the Word with the humanity of Christ and other mysteries of the Redemption which cause the Baptist to marvel and reflect on them saying

"What mystery is this? What presentiments of happiness? From the moment when I recognized my Lord in my Mother's womb, I have not felt such stirring of my soul as now! Is it possible that He is now happily come? That he Saviour of the world is now near me?"

Jesus Is Baptised In The Jordan

The wide shallow riverbed of the Jordan slowly carries its blue waters southwards, the greenish tint in the water at the edges arising from the lush green vegetation growing in the humid soil of the low riverbanks. The movement of the water is just enough to avoid the formation of marshes, its smooth flow testament to the flatness of the riverbed also reflected in the vast flat and arid country on the far-left- side of the river Jordan that is the desert of Judah; empty wasteland strewn with stones and rubble like alluvial grounds after a flood. There are no houses in sight and no cultivated fields but here and there, a few shrubs grow in clusters where the soil is less parched.

Here on the right bank of the river, in the neighbourhood of Bethany, also known as Betharaba, there is a great peace, special and unusual, as of a place full of the memories of angels flapping their wings and of heavenly voices, a place that communicates with the soul.

Slowly, a crowd gathers on the right riverbank; men from all walks of life, dressed in different fashions; some ordinary, some rich, and some Pharisees wearing tunics adorned with fringes and braids.

In the midst of the crowd, standing on a rock podium, is a tall, dark man in a Carmel hair garment giving a sermon in a voice like a thunderbolt. It is John the Baptist, the Precursor, and his sermon is severe as with his words, his tone and his gestures, he announces the coming of the Messiah, urging the people to prepare their hearts, breakdown barriers and correct their thoughts. It is a violent and harsh sermon delivered like a doctor who lays a wound bare, scrutinises it and then cuts it mercilessly.

On an ancient, well-trodden narrow path that runs parallel to the strip of green shrub on this bank, Jesus, alone, walking slowly and noiselessly, approaches the Baptist from behind, listening to the thundering voice of the Penitent of the desert, just like one of the many who come to John to be baptised and purified for the coming of the Messiah. Jesus' clothes are those of common people but His looks are the perfection of physical handsomeness and His bearing is that of a gentleman. But there is nothing divine, that is immediately obvious, to distinguish Him from the others.

But a special spirituality must emanate from Him that John perceives because he turns around and immediately identifies its source. Impulsively, John comes down from his podium and hastens towards Jesus, Who has stopped a few yards away from the crowd and is leaning against a tree trunk. Today is the thirtieth day after His thirtieth birthday.

The two men stare at one another; Jesus, with His very sweet blue eyes, John with his very severe flashing feverish black ones. Both men are tall but the resemblance ends there; whilst Jesus looks majestic in His simple tunic, wears His fair hair long and tidy, framing His white ivory face, John's straight black hair falls unevenly onto his shoulders and his sparse dark beard covers his face almost completely, his cheeks are hallowed by fasting, his complexion dark, tanned and weather beaten by the sun and dry conditions of living in the desert, and his hairy body half- naked in his camel hair garment that covers his trunk down to his thin sides and is tied at the waist with a leather belt, leaving his right side bare and completely weather beaten. In appearance, one is the antithesis of the other; like a savage and an angel.

'Here is the Lamb of God!...' John exclaims after his
scrutiny. And bowing down before Jesus, he adds
''...How is it that my lord comes to me?'

'To fulfil the penitential rite' replies Jesus, calmly.

'Never, my Lord. I must come to You to be sanctified,
and You are coming to me?'

' Let it be done as I wish....' says Jesus, laying His hand on John's bowed head '...so that all justice may be fulfilled and that your rite may become the beginning of a higher mystery...And men may be informed that the victim is in the world.

John looks at Jesus with eyes now sweetened by tears and then leads the way back to the river-bank where Jesus takes off His mantle and tunic. Wearing only a pair of shorts, Jesus wades into the shallow waters of the river Jordan where, using a cup made from an emptied dried pumpkin shell which he keeps tied to his belt, John pours some water from the river onto Jesus' head, baptising Him. In this moment, the Heavens open and a divine Dove descends upon Him Who is to baptise men with that Dove, and an announcement, more powerful than the angel's is heard descending from Heaven, from the eternal Father:

"This is My beloved Son, in Whom I am well pleased."

Many of the bystanders hear this voice including even those who are not worthy of such favour and they also see the Holy Ghost descending upon the Saviour because this manifestation is given without reserve.

White, meek and modest, the Lamb of God climbs back onto the riverbank, puts on His clothes and then concentrates in prayer whilst John points Him out to the crowd telling them that he recognised Him by the sign that the Spirit of God had shown him as the infallible means to identify the Redeemer

This is the third manifestation of Christ to the world after His birth; through the Magi, Simeon at the Temple and now through the Baptist.

Over the next three years, Jesus' fatherland will be strewn with His manifestations like seed scattered to the four winds; in every social condition and class, down to the last ones: His Resurrection and Ascension into Heaven: to shepherds and powerful people, scholars and sceptics, Jews and Gentiles, priests and sinners, rulers, soldiers and children.

And they continue, even now. But, as in the past, the world will not accept the present manifestations and will forget the past ones. But Jesus says He will not give up; He will repeat Himself to save men, to persuade them to have faith in Him, no longer confining Himself to words, which tire and detach men, but resorting to visions, also, to make His Gospel clear, giving everybody the possibility of knowing Him.

And if, like cruel children, they should throw away the gift without understanding its value, then they will be left with His indignation.

Then, says Jesus:'...I shall be able to once again

repeat the old reproach: "We played for you and you would not dance; we sang dirges and you would not weep." But it does not matter. Let them, the inconvertible ones, heap burning coals on their heads...'

Jesus Is Tempted In The Desert By The Devil

Deep into the arid desert that lies on the left side of the river Jordan, there is nothing but solitude, stones and such parched earth that it has become a yellowish dust that rises now and again in small wind currents, into small eddies that are hot and dry like breath from a feverish mouth. The eddies are very troublesome as they readily penetrate the nostrils and throat of anyone in this hostile place.

Despite the odds, a few small thorny bushes, survive in the desolation, sparsely scattered here and there like small random forelocks of surviving hair on a bald head. Overhead, the sky is mercilessly blue. On the ground; arid land, stones and silence.

Inside a rock grotto formed out of huge overhanging rock, Jesus is sitting on a stone that has been taken into the cave, leaning against a piece of the rock that overhangs; out of the scorching sun. For the past forty days, the stone on which He now sits has also been his kneeling stool and his pillow when He takes a few hours rest, enveloped in His mantle beneath the starry sky, in the chill air of the night. By His side, the knapsack He brought with Him when He departed from Nazareth lies empty. Jesus Himself is very thin and pale.

Extract from 'The Mystical City of God'
By Venerable Mary of Jesus of Agreda.

The forty days of His fast have been offered to the Father in satisfaction of the vice of gluttony just as He will conquer each vice by the exercise of the virtues contrary to them; profound humility for pride, voluntary poverty and total privation for avarice, penance and austerity for lust, meekness and charity towards His enemies for vengeful anger, ceaseless labours for laziness and negligence, upright sincerity, truthfulness and loving interactions for envy and deceit.

For each of the forty days, He makes three hundred genuflections and prays in praise and thanksgiving to the Father, prostrate on the ground in the form of a cross.

Back in Nazareth, as soon as Mary learns that Jesus is on His way to the desert, She too retires to Her room, so completely, that Her neighbours think She had departed with Jesus. She begins Her fast at the same time s Jesus and also fasts for forty days, copying Him in every action and in sync; genuflections, prostrations and prayers of praise and thanksgiving, seeing and communicating with Him by their unique and special interior science and also through their angel messengers.

Until the thirty fifth day of the fast, Christ tempers all attempts by Satan and his crew to discover the true source of His infinite power showing just enough to prove that He, Christ, is a man so far advanced in holiness as to gain these powers. But as the time approaches for Him to enter into battle and crush Satan's pride and malice, He offers a prayer to the Father in preparation and hides His angels from Satan's sight.

His battle with Satan begins on the thirty-fifth day of His fast and lasts five days. Satan's main mission is to establish once and for all whether or not Jesus is indeed the Christ-the Son of God, the same God-Man that he, Lucifer, when still in possession of his angelic beauty, had refused to know and revere as his chief. If he could establish this fact then he would also find the Woman, the Mother of the Incarnate Word who was destined to vanquish him. To this end, Satan and his Legions, Made bold by their own arrogance, strain all their power and malice, lashing themselves into a fury against the superior strength which they find in Jesus.

DAY 1

Sitting with His elbows resting on His knees, forearms forward, hands joined and fingers interlaced, Jesus is meditating. Now and again, He looks up and around, then looks at the sun that is now almost perpendicular in the blue sky. Then He closes His eyes and leans on the rock as one seized by a dizzy spell.

Then Satan appears enveloped in a Bedouin robe and a large mantle shaped like a domino- a huge cloak worn with a mask. His ugly face appears framed by the white flaps of the Bedouin turban he is wearing on his head. The flaps fall down his cheeks, onto his shoulders leaving only a small dark triangle of his face with thin sinuous lips and deep, jet black magnetic eyes that would penetrate and read the depths of one's soul but in which one can read nothing. Or mystery. They stab and burn your soul.

He is the very opposite of Jesus in whose beautiful bright blue eyes, also magnetic and penetrating to the depth of the soul, one can read love and bounty. They caress and heal.

Satan begins with a **sensual seduction** cloaked in a
simple act of kindness that very quickly degenerates...

'Are you alone?' asks Satan, approaching Jesus.

Jesus looks at him but says nothing.

'How did you happen to be here? Did you get lost?'

Jesus looks at him again but remains silent.

'If I had water in my flask, I would give you some. But I have none myself. My horse died and I am now going on foot to the ford. I will get a drink there, and find someone who will give me some bread. ...I know the road. Come with me, I'll take you there.'

This time, Jesus does not even look at him.

'You do not answer; do You know that if You stay here You will die? The wind is starting to rise. There will be a storm. Come'

Jesus clenches His hands in silent prayer.

'Ah! It is You then? I have been looking for You for such a long time! And I have been watching You for so long. Since You were baptised. Are You calling the Eternal? He is far away. You are now on the earth, in the midst of men. And I reign over men. And yet, I feel sorry for You, and I want to help You because You are so good, and You have come to sacrifice Yourself for nothing...'

And Satan sits down in front of Jesus, scrutinises Him with his dreadful eyes and smiles at Him with his snakelike mouth. But Jesus remains silent and in prayer.

Extract from 'The Mystical City of God'
By Venerable Mary of Jesus of Agreda.

'...Men will hate You because of Your goodness. They understand nothing but gold, food and pleasure. Sacrifice, sorrow and obedience are words more arid to them than the land around us here ... more arid than this dust. Only snakes hide here waiting to bite, and jackals waiting to tear to pieces-
-Come with me; It is not worthwhile suffering for them. I know them better than You do.'

But Jesus continues to pray.

The strain for Satan and his legions is very much on establishing the identity of this Person; Is He just a holy man or is He the Christ? To do this, they must break the shield that prevents them from knowing the true source of his power...

... but the strength proves too much for them and the distraction unsuccessful

End of extract

DAY 2

on the second day, Satan appears clothed in light like an angel and without much formality, proceeds with a new proposition, tempting **lust**.

'You don't trust me but You are wrong. I am the wisdom of the earth. I can be Your teacher and show You how to triumph. See? The important thing is to triumph-
- Once we have imposed ourselves and enchanted the world, then we can take them wherever we want. But first, we must be as they wish us to be. Like them. We must allure them, make them believe we admire them and follow their thoughts-

- You are young and handsome. Start with a woman; one must always start from her. I made a mistake inducing her to be disobedient. I should have advised her differently. I would have turned her into a better instrument and I would have beaten God. I was in a hurry-

-But You! I will teach You because one day, I looked at You with angelical joy and a fraction of that love is still left in me but You must listen to me and make use of my experience. Find Yourself a woman; where You do not succeed, she will. You are the new Adam: You must have Your Eve-

- In any case, how can You understand and heal the diseases of the senses if You do not know what they are? Don't You know that, that is where the seed is, from which the tree of greediness and arrogance sprouts?

Why do men want to reign? Why do they want to be rich and powerful?...To possess a woman; She is like a lark, only attracted by sparkling things. Gold and power are two sides of the mirror that draws woman, and are the cause of evil in the world... Look: out of a thousand different crimes, at least nine hundred take root from the lust of possessing a woman or in the passion of a woman burning with desire that man has not yet satisfied or can no longer satisfy. Go to a woman if You want to know what life is. And only then will You be able to cure and heal the diseases of mankind-

-Women, You know, are beautiful! There is nothing nicer in the world. Man has brains and strength. But woman! Her thought is a perfume, her touch the caress of flowers, her grace like wine; pleasant to drink, her weakness like a coil of silk or a child's curl in a man's hand, her caress, a strength poured over our own strength and inflames it. Sorrow, fatigue, worries are forgotten when we lie near a woman and she is in our arms like a bunch of flowers-

Jesus makes no answer and continues to pray.

DAY 3

Frustrated by his lack of progress Satan strives with his cunning to drive at the heart of the matter. Still clothed in light, he conjectures that Christ must be hungry and then cunningly rests his advice on the **supposition of His being the Son of God**.

- But what a fool I am! You are hungry and I am talking to You of women. You are exhausted, that is why that fragrance of the earth, that flower of creation, the fruit that gives and excites love, seems without value to You...But look at these stones. How round and smooth they look, gilded by the setting sun! Don't they look like loaves? ...Since You're the Son of God, all You have to say is: "I want" and they will become sweet smelling bread, just like the loaves housewives are now taking out of their ovens for the super of their families...And these arid acacias, if You only wish so, will they not be filled with sweet fruit and dates as sweet as honey? Eat Your fill, Son of God. You are the Master of the earth. The earth is bowing down to put itself at Your feet and appease Your hunger.

-Don't You see how You turn pale and unsteady at the mention of bread? Poor Jesus! Are You so weak that You cannot even work a miracle? Shall I work it

for You? I am not Your equal, but I can do
something. I will do without any strength for a whole
year, gather it all together, but I want to serve You,
because You are good and I always remember that
You are my God, even if now I have forfeited the right
to call You so. Help me with Your prayers, that I
may...'

'Be quiet! "Man does not live on bread alone, but on
every word that comes from the mouth of God."'

Satan starts with anger, grinds his teeth and clenches
his fists but he controls himself and turns his
grinning into a smile, not wishing to show any
weakness or to exit the contest.

DAY 4

Rousing his courage by his arrogance, Satan returns with yet another proposition, this time with the aim of arousing **vanity** in Jesus...

'I understand. You are above the necessities of the earth and You are disgusted at making use of me. I deserved that.....But come and see what there is in the House of God. I will take You up to the pinnacle of the Temple where You will see how even priests do not refuse to come to a compromise between the spirit and the flesh; after all, they are men and not angels ...'

Christ permits Himself to be physically carried to the pinnacle of the Temple in Jerusalem, from where they can observe multitudes of people though they themselves were unseen.

'...Work a spiritual miracle; undergo a transfiguration and become most handsome. Then, call a host of angels and tell them to form a footrest for Your feet with their wings interlaced, and to let You down thus into the main yard so that people may see You and remember that God exists. One must show oneself now and again because man's memory is so weak particularly with regard to spiritual matters. You can imagine how happy the angels will be to form a protection for Your feet and a ladder for You to descend!'

'It is said: "You must not put the Lord your God to the test."'

'You understand that Your apparition would change nothing and the Temple would continue to be a market full of corruption. Your divine wisdom is aware that the hearts of ministers of the Temple are nests of vipers that tear and are torn to pieces for the sake of success. They are subdued only by human power-

Day 5

Extract from 'The Mystical City of God'
By Venerable Mary of Jesus of Agreda.

Having failed in his fourth attempt, Satan now seeks
to rouse the Saviour's **ambition** for a share in 'his
dominion'...

For this, Jesus permits Satan to take Him up to a
very high mount from where they can see across
many lands and after showing Him all the sights and
the wealth, where Satan, with exorbitant boldness
rather more like madness, Satan promises what he
does not possess nor ever will possess in exchange for
the one thing he craves the most...

End of extract

- Well then, come. Adore me. I will give You the earth.
Alexander, Cyrus, Caesar, all the great rulers, past or
present, will be like the leaders of miserable caravans
when compared to You, as You shall have the
kingdoms of the world under Your sceptre. And with
the kingdoms, all the wealth, all the beautiful things
on earth; women, horses, armies and temples. You
will be able to raise Your sign everywhere when You
are the King of kings and the Lord of the world. Then
You will be obeyed and respected both by the people

and by the priesthood. All classes will honour and serve You, because You will be the powerful One, the Only One, the Lord.

- Adore me for one moment only! Appease this thirst of mine for being worshipped! It ruined me but it is still left in me and I am parched by it. The flames of hell are like a fresh morning breeze compared to this fierce passion burning inside me. It is my hell, this thirst...One moment, one moment only, Christ...'

And Satan falls on his knees imploring:

'...You are so good! One moment of joy for the eternally Tortured One! Let me feel what it is like to be god and I will be Your devoted , obedient servant for all Your life and all Your enterprises...One instant, one instant only and I will no longer torture You!'

Instead, Jesus stands taller, His face terribly severe and potent His eyes, two burning sapphires. He has lost weight from the long days of fasts and now looks even taller and His voice, like thunder, reverberates when he cries:

"Be off, Satan! It is written: "You must worship the Lord Your God and serve Him alone."

With a cry of dreadful torture and indescribable hatred, Satan springs to his feet, a dreadful furious smoky figure, and disappears with a last cursing yell.

After this fifth day, Christ suspends the permission for Lucifer to tempt him further and hurls him and his legions into the caverns of hell where they find themselves entirely crushed and unable to move for three days and still non-the-wiser about whether or not He who had crushed them so badly is the Incarnate Word or not, and in such uncertainty they remain until during the Crucifixion on Calvary

In triumphal songs of praise and thanks to the Father for this victory over the enemy of God and man, the angels bear Jesus back to the desert here, tired, He sits down and leans back with His head resting on the stone. He is perspiring and looks exhausted but angels come to blow gently with their wings in the uncomfortable humidity of the cave, purifying and refreshing it the air. Jesus opens His eyes and smiles, seemingly nourished and reinvigorated by the aroma of Paradise.

The sun has set in the west. He takes his knapsack and in the company of the angels who, flying above His head, emit a mild light as darkness quickly approaches, walks steady in the north- east direction. He now assumed His usual expression and the only remaining sign of His long fast is a more ascetic look on His thin, pale face and His eyes enraptured in a joy which does not belong to this world.

Jesus Meets John And James

Returning from the desert, Jesus, once again, is walking along the green strip of vegetation on the banks of the river Jordan, near to the place where He was baptised, which is also a well-known ford used for crossing over from Bethany to Perea. The place is now deserted, but for a few travellers on foot, some riding donkeys and others horses.

Jesus proceeds on His way northwards, absorbed in thought and seemingly unaware of the travellers. When He reaches the ford, He meets a group of men of varying ages, discussing animatedly, perhaps about the arrest of the Baptist the day before, and then they part company and disperse in different directions; some southwards and others northwards.

Two brothers, John and James, are amongst those heading North and having first sported Jesus, John points Him out to his brother and companions. They talk a little amongst themselves and then John peels off from the group and walks quickly towards Jesus. James follows him, walking a little slower. The others, showing no interest, continue with their discussion, also walking slowly.

When John is about two or three metres from Jesus, He shouts: ' Lamb of God Who takes away the sins of the world!'

Jesus turns round and looks at him. There are now only a few steps between them. They look at each other: Jesus with his serious scrutinising look, John with his pure smiling eyes in his beautiful youthful face that looks like the face of a girl. He is about twenty years old, beardless, with only the sign of blond down like a golden veil on his rosy cheeks.

"Who are you looking for?' asks Jesus.

'For You, Master.'

'How do you know I am a Master?'

'The Baptist told me.'

'Well then, why do you call Me Lamb?'

'Because I heard him call You so one day when You were passing by, just over a month ago.'

'What do You want from Me?'

'I want You to tell us words of eternal life and to comfort us.'

'But who are you?'

'I am John of Zebedee, and this is my brother James. We are fishermen from Galilee. But we are also disciples of John. He spoke words of life to us and we listened to him because we want to follow God, and deserve His forgiveness doing penance and thus prepare our hearts for the coming of the Messiah. You are the Messiah. John said so, because he saw the sign of the Dove descending on You. He said to us: "Here is the Lamb of God." I say to You: Lamb of God Who takes away the sins of the world, give us peace because we no longer have anyone who may guide us,

and our souls are upset."'
'Where is John?'
'Herod has taken him. He is in prison at Machaerus.
The most faithful amongst his disciples have tried to
free him but it is not possible. We are coming from
there. Let us come with You Master, show us where
You live.'
'Come. But do you know what you are asking for?
Who follows me, will have to leave everything: his
home, his relatives, his way of thinking, also his life. I
will make you My disciples and My friends if you wish
but I have neither wealth nor protection. I am poor,
and I shall be even poorer, to the extent of not having
a place where I may rest My head. And I will be
persecuted by My enemies, even more than a lost
sheep is persecuted by wolves. My doctrine is even
more rigid than John's because it also forbids
resentment, and is concerned not so much with
external matters but with the soul...You must be
reborn if you want to be My disciples. Are you willing
to do that?'
'Yes, Master. Only You have words that can give us
light. They descend upon us and where there was
darkness and desolation because we had no guide,
they shed light and sunshine.'
'Come, then, let us go. I will teach you on our way.'
And so, together, they go back to the shores of Lake
Galilee where John and James, spend a day in the
hospitality of a friend of Jesus's relatives.

John And James Speak To Peter About The Messiah

It is a very clear dawn over the Lake of Galilee; the Sky and the water sparkle with rosy flashes similar to the mild ones on the walls of the little orchards of the lake-village where fruit trees rise from the orchards and bend with unkempt foliage peeping into the lanes.

The village is starting to stir with women going to the fountain or to the washing place, fishermen unloading baskets of fish or haggling over prices in very loud voices. The village is quite large and spread along the lake.

Coming out of a little street, John walks quickly towards the lake, calmly followed by James. At the lake, John scans over the boats already ashore and not seeing the one he is looking for, he turns his gaze over the lake and spots the boat about a hundred yards from the beach, manoeuvring its way into the harbour. Holding his hands by the sides of his mouth to project his voice, he calls, extending the note, at the top of his voice:

"Oh-e!"
When he gets their attention, he gesticulates with both arms to say 'Come, come.'

Not knowing what it is about, the men on the boat lay on the oars and the boat speeds up. When they are about ten metres away from the shore, John, not wanting to wait any longer, takes off his mantle, his long tunic and his sandals and throws them on the shore. Then lifting his under tunic and holding it with one hand against his groin, he wades into the water to meet the arriving boat.

'Why did you two not come?' asks Andrew whilst Peter
sulks silently.

'And why did you not come with me and James?'
John replies to Andrew.
'I went fishing. I have no time to waste. You
disappeared with that man...'
'I beckoned to you to come. It is Him. You should hear
His words! We stayed with Him all day until late at
night. We have now come to say to you: "Come."'
'Is it really Him? Are you sure? We only saw Him
then, when the Baptist pointed Him out to us.'
'It is Him. He did not deny it.'
'Anyone can say whatever suits him to impose himself
on dupes. It is not the first time...' grumbles Peter.
'Oh Simon! Don't say that! He is the Messiah! He
knows everything! He hears you.' admonishes John,
grieved and dismayed.
'Sure! The Messiah! And He showed Himself to you,
James and Andrews! Three poor fishermen! ...' mocks
Peter. '...The Messiah will need much more than that!
...And He hears me! Eh! My poor boy. The first spring
sunshine has damaged your brains! Come on, come
and do some work. That's much better. And forget
such fairy tales!'
'I'm telling you, He is the Messiah! John said holy
things but He speaks of God. Who is not Christ
cannot speak such words.'
'Simon, I am not a boy. I am old enough and I am
composed and thoughtful. You know that...' pleads
James. '...I did not speak much but I listened a lot
during the hours we spent with the Lamb of God and
I can tell you that really He can but be the Messiah!
Why don't you believe? Why do you not want to

believe? Perhaps because you have not heard Him but I believe Him. We are poor and ignorant? Well, He says that He has come to announce the Gospel of the kingdom of God and of the Kingdom of peace to the poor, humble and little ones before the great ones...He said: "The great ones already have their delights. They are not enviable delights when compared with the ones I have come to bring you. The great ones are already capable of understanding by means of their culture. But I have come to the 'little' ones of Israel and of the world, to those who weep and hope, to those who seek Light and are hungry for the real Manna, to whom learned men do not give light and food, but only burdens, darkness, chains, contempt...And I call the 'little ones'. I have come to turn the world upside down because I will lower what is now held high and raise what is now held in contempt...let those who want the truth and peace, who want eternal life, come to Me...Those who love light, let them come to Me...I am the Light of the world."...Did He not say that John?'
'Yes. And He said: "The world will not love Me. The great world will not love Me because it is corrupted by vices and idolatry. Nay, the world will not want Me, because it is the offspring of Darkness and so does not love the Light...But the earth is not only made of the great world, but also those who, mixed with the world, are not of the world. There are people who are of the world because they have been imprisoned in it, like fish in a net." ...He said exactly that because we were speaking on the shore of the lake and He

pointed at some nets that were being dragged ashore with fish in them. Nay, He said: "See. None of those fish wanted to be caught in the net. Also, men would not intentionally like to fall prey to Mammon. Not even the most wicked, who blinded by pride, do not believe they have no right to do what they do. Their real sin is pride. All the other sins grow from it.
...Those who are not completely wicked, would like falling prey to Mammon even less. But they fall because they are frivolous and because of a weight that drags them to the bottom, which is Adam's sin...I have come to remove that sin, and while awaiting the hour of Redemption, to give those who believe in Me, strength that will enable them to free themselves from the snares that trap them and thus make them free to follow Me, the Light of the world."

'Well then, if He said that, we must go to Him at once.' says Peter, impulsive but genuine, hastening to unload the boat now beached ashore. They unload nets, ropes and sails...'And you, silly Andrew, why did you not go with them?!...'
'But...Simon! You reproached me because I did not persuade them to come with me...You have been grumbling all night, and now, you rebuke me because I did not go?!'
'You're right...But I did not see Him...you did...and you must have seen that He is not like us.....He must have something compelling!...'
'Oh! Yes.' says John. 'His face! His eyes! What

beautiful eyes, aren't they James?! And His
voice!....Oh! What a voice! When He speaks, you seem
to be dreaming of Heaven.'
'Quick, quick. Let's go and see Him' says Peter eagerly
and then addressing the other fishermen, he says '
Take everything to Zebedee and tell him to do as he
thinks best. We will be back this evening in time to go
fishing.'

They all get dressed and set out but Peter stops after
a few yards, grasp hold of John's hand and asks ' Did
you say he knows everything and hears everything?...'
'Yes, I did. Just think: When we saw the moon high in
the sky last night, I said: "I wonder what Simon would
be doing right now", and He said: "He is casting his
net and he cannot set his mind at rest because he
has to do it all my himself since you did not go out
with the twin boat on such a good evening for
fishing...he does not know that before long, he will be
fishing with different nets and catching different fish.'
'Holy Mercy! It's true! Well, He will also have
heard...also that I called Him little less than a liar...I
can't go to Him!'
'Oh! He is so good. He certainly knows what you
thought. He already knew because when we told Him
we were coming to you, He said: "Go. But don't let the
first words of contempt discourage you. Who wants to
come to Me must be able to make headway against
the sneering words of the world and the prohibitions
of relatives. Because I am above blood and society
and I triumph over them. And who is with Me will

also triumph forever."....He also said: Don't be afraid to speak. The man who hears will come, because he is a man of goodwill."

'Is that what He said? Well, I'll come. Speak, speak of Him while we are going. Where is He?'

'In a poor house; they must be His friends.'

'Is He poor?'

'A workman from Nazareth, so He said.'

'And how does He live now if He no longer works?'

'We did not ask Him. Perhaps, His relatives help Him.'

'It would have been better if we had brought some fish, some bread and fruit...something. We are going to consult a rabbi,...because He is like....He is more than a rabbi and we are going empty-handed! Our rabbis don't like that...'

'But He does. We had but twenty pennies between us, James and I, and we offered them to Him, as is customary with rabbis but He did not want them. But since we insisted so much, He said: "May God reward you with the blessings of the poor. Come with Me" and He gave them to some poor people: He knew where they lived. And when we asked Him: Master, are You not keeping anything for Yourself?" He replied: "The joy of doing the will of God and serving His glory...We also said: You are calling us, Master, but we are all poor, what shall we bring You?" He answered with a smile that brought us enjoyment of the delights of Paradise: "I want a great treasure from you",..and we said "But we have nothing" and He answered: *"A treasure with seven names, which* *even the poorest may have whilst the rich have not. You have it, and I want it. Listen to the names: Charity, faith, goodwill, right intention, continence*, sincerity, spirit of sacrifice.* That is what I want from My followers. Only that. And you have it...it is dormant, like seed under a winter clod, but the spring sunshine will make it sprout into a sevenfold spike." That is what He said.'

'Ah! Now I feel that He is a true Rabboni, the promised Messiah! He is not harsh with the poor, He does not ask for money...It is enough to call Him the holy man of God. We can go safely.'

*Continence is the exercise of self-restraint in sensual matters such as food, drink, comfort, image and lusts as well as over other matters of flesh, the mind and its desires, the heart and its passions.

First Meeting Of Peter And The Messiah

Jesus, alone, is walking along a path between two fields, in a direction opposite to that of

John is hurrying along a path in the fields, his blond-brown hair undulating at each step. His face is rosy and beardless, the fair complexion of a youth, hardly a man. There is no sign of a moustache, only the smoothness of his rosy cheeks, his red lips, and his bright smile. He has a pure look because of the clarity of his virginal soul that shines through his turquoise blue eyes.

Jesus, alone on a separate path between two fields, is walking in the opposite direction.

When John is about to pass through the hedge, he shouts 'Master!'

Jesus stops and turns round, smiling.

'Master, I have longed so much for You!' The people in the house where You live told me You had come towards the country but they did not say where. I was afraid I might not meet You' says John, his head slightly bowed, respectfully. His attitude and his eyes are full of truthful love and whilst he speaks, with his head still inclined towards his shoulder, he raises his turquoise eyes towards Jesus.

'I saw you were looking for Me and I came towards you.'

'You saw me? Where were You Master?'
'Over there' and He points to a cluster of olive trees far away. 'I was over there. I was praying and reflecting on what to say this evening in the synagogue. But I came away as soon as I saw you.'
'But how could You see me, if I can hardly see the place, hidden as it is behind the hedge?'
'And yet, you see, here I am. I came to meet you because I saw you. What the eye does not do, love does.'
'Yes, love does. You love me therefore, Master?'
'And do you love me, John, son of Zebedee?'
'So much, Master. I think I have always loved You. Before meeting You, long before, my soul was looking for You, and when I saw You, my soul said to me: "Here is the One you are seeking". I think I met You because my soul perceived You.'

'You said it, John, and what you say is right. I also came towards you because My soul perceived you.

For how long will you love me?'

'Forever, Master. I no longer want to love anybody but You.'

'You have a father and a mother, brothers and sisters, you have your life, and with your life, you have a woman and love. How will you be able to leave all that for my sake?'

'Master...I do not know...but I think, if it is not pride to say so, that Your fondness will take the place of father and mother, brothers and sisters and also of a woman. I will be compensated for everything if You love me.'

'And if My love should cause you sorrows and persecutions?'

'They will be nothing if You love me.'

'And the day I should die...'

'No! You are young, Master...why die?'

'Because the Messiah has come to preach the Law in its truthfulness and to accomplish Redemption. And the world loathes the Law and does not want Redemption. Therefore they persecute God's messengers.'

'Oh! Let that never be! Do not mention that prediction of death to him who loves You! ....But if You should die, I would still love You. Allow me to love You.' John implores, his head now bowed lower than ever as he walks beside Jesus.

Jesus stops and scrutinises him with His deep penetrating eyes and then lays His hand on John's bowed head ' I want you to love me .'

'Oh! Master! 'exhales John happily, his eyes shining

with tears, his shapely mouth smiling. He takes and kisses the back of the divine hand and presses it to his heart. They move on again.

'You said you were looking for Me...'

'Yes, to tell You that my friends want to meet You... And because, oh! How I was longing to be with You again! I left You only a few hours ago... but I could no longer be without You.'

'Have you therefore been a good announcer of the Word?'

'Also James, Master, spoke of You in such a way as... to convince them.'

'So, also he who had no confidence- and is not to be blamed because his reserve was due to prudence- is now convinced. Let us go and give them full assurance.'

'He was somewhat afraid...'

'No! Not afraid of Me! I have come for good people and even more for those who stand in error. I want to save people, not condemn them. I will be full of mercy with honest people.'

'And with sinners?'

'Also. By dishonest people, I mean those who are spiritually dishonest and hypocritically feign to be good whilst they do ill deeds. And they do them for their own profit, in order to secure an advantage over their neighbours. I will be severe with them.'

'Oh! Simon needs not worry then. He is as loyal as no one else '

'That is what I like, and I want you all to be so.'

'Simon wants to tell You many things.'
'I will listen to him after speaking in the synagogue. I asked them to inform the poor and sick people in addition to the rich and healthy ones. They are all in need of the Gospel.'

Near the village, they meet some children playing on the road. One of the children runs into Jesus' legs and would have fallen had Jesus not been quick to get hold of him. The child cries just the same, as though he had been hurt and Jesus, holding him in his arms, says ' An Israelite crying?' what should the thousands of children have done, who became men crossing the desert with Moses? And the Most High Lord sent sweet manna for them because He loves innocent children and looks after these little angels of the earth, these wingless little birds, just as He sees to the sparrows of woods and towns. Do you like honey? Yes? Well, if you are good, you will eat honey which is sweeter than the honey of your bees.'
'Where? When?'
'When, after a life of loyalty to God, you will go to Him.'
' I know that I cannot go there unless the Messiah comes. My mother says that now, we in Israel, are like many Moses and we die seeing the Promised Land. She says that we are there, waiting to go in, and that only the Messiah will make us go in.'
'What a clever little Israelite! Well, I tell you, that when you die, you will go to Paradise at once because the Messiah would already have opened the gates of

Heaven. But You must be good.'

'Mummy! Mummy!....'cries the child, sliding down from Jesus' arms and then running to a young woman, who is going into her house, carrying a copper amphora.'...Mummy! The new Rabbi told me that I will go to Paradise at once when I die and I will eat so much honey.....If I am good. I will be good!'

'God grant it! I am sorry, Master, if he troubled You. He is so lively!'

'Innocence does not trouble, woman. May God bless you because you are a woman who is bringing her children up in the knowledge of the Law.'

The woman blushes at the praise. 'May the blessing of the Lord be with You too.' She replies and then she disappears with her little one.

'Do you like children, Master?'

'Yes, I do, because they are pure...sincere...and affectionate.'

'Have You any nephews Master?'

'I have but My Mother...In Her, there is purity, sincerity, the love of the most holy children, together with wisdom, justice and the fortitude of adults. I have everything in My Mother, John.'

'And You left Her?'

'God is above, also, the holiest mother.'

'Will I meet Her?'

'Yes, you will.'

'And will She love me?'

'She will love you because She loves whoever loves Her Jesus.'

'Then, You have no brothers?'

'I have some cousins on My Mother's husband's side.
But every man is My brother, and I have come for
everybody. Here we are now, at the synagogue. I am
going in and you will join Me with your friends.'

John goes away and Jesus enters the synagogue, a
square room with a display of triangular lamps,
lecterns and rolls of parchment and a crowd waiting
and praying. Jesus also prays. The crowd whispers
behind Him as He bows to the head of the synagogue,
greets him and asks for a roll at random.

Then He begins His lesson:

"The Spirit makes Me read the following to you from
Jeremiah 7:"Yahweh Sabaoth, the God of Israel, says
this: Amend your behaviour and your actions and I
will stay with you here in this place. Put no trust in
delusive words like these: This is the Sanctuary of
Yahweh! The Sanctuary of Yahweh, the Sanctuary of
Yahweh! But if you do amend your behaviour and
your actions, if you treat each other fairly, if you do
not exploit the stranger, the orphan and the widow, if
you do not shed innocent blood in this place and if
you do not follow alien gods, to your own ruin, then
here, in this place, I will stay with you, in the land
that long ago I gave to your father forever'".

Listen, Israel. Here I am to illuminate for you the
words of light, which your dimmed souls can no
longer see or understand. Listen. There is much

weeping in the land of the People of God: old people cry remembering past glories, adults cry because they are bent under the yoke, children cry because they have no prospects of future glory. But the glory of the earth is nothing compared to a glory which no oppressor, except Mammon and ill will, can take away.

Why are you crying? Because the Most High, Who was always good to His people, has turned His face elsewhere and no longer allows His children to see His Face. Is He not the God Who parted the sea, made Israel cross it, led them through the desert, fed them and defended them from their enemies ...and that they might not lose the way to Heaven, He gave them a Law for their souls as He sent them a cloud for their bodies? ...Is He no longer the God That sweetened the waters and sent manna to His worn out children? Is He not the God Who wanted you to settle in His land and made alliance with you as Father with His children? Well, then, why has the foreigner struck you?

Many amongst you mumble: "And yet the temple is here!" It is not enough to have the Temple and to go and pray God in it. The first temple is in the heart of everyman and that is where holy prayers should be said... But a prayer cannot be holy unless the heart first amends its way of living and with His heart, man also amends his habits, affections, the rules of justice towards the poor, servants, relatives and God.

Now look. I see rich hard-hearted men who make rich offerings to the Temple but never say to a poor man:" Brother, here is a piece of bread, and a penny. Take them, from man to man, and let not my help discourage you as my offering may not make me proud." ...I see people who in their prayers, complain to God because He does not hear their prayers promptly; then, when a poor wretch, very often a relative, says to them:" Listen to me" heartlessly, they reply "No"...I see you crying because your money is squeezed out of your pockets by your ruler. But then, you squeeze blood out of those you hate and you are not filled with horror when you take the blood and life away from a body.

O Israel! The time of Redemption has come. Prepare its ways in your hearts with good will. Be honest...good...love one another...The rich must not despise the poor, merchants must not defraud...the poor must not envy the rich. You are all of one blood and you belong to one God...You are all called to one destiny. Do not shut, with your sins, the Heavens that the Messiah will open for you. Have you erred so far? Err no longer. Abandon all errors.

The law is simple, easy and good as it goes back to the original Ten Commandments, illuminated by the light of love. Come. I will show you which they are: love, love, love. God's love for you. Your love for God.

Love for your neighbours. Always love, because God is love and those are the father's children who know how to live love.

I am here for every body and to give everybody the light of God. Here is the word of the Father that becomes food for you. Come, taste, change the blood of your spirits with this food. Let every poison vanish, let every lust die. A new glory is offered to you: the eternal one, to which all those will come whose hearts will truly study the Law of God.

Start from love, there is nothing greater. When you know how to love, you will already know everything, and God will love you, and God's love means help against all temptations. May the blessing of God be to those who turn to God with their hearts full of good will."

Jesus is silent. The people whisper. Then they sing hymns, many of which are psalms, before they break up.

Jesus exits onto the little square and finds John, James, Peter and Andrew waiting at the doorstep.

'Peace to you...'greets Jesus'...Here is the man who in

order to be just, must not judge before knowing, but is honest in admitting he is wrong. Simon, you wanted to see Me? Here I am. And you, Andrew, why did you not come before?'

The two brothers look at each other, embarrassed, and then Andrew whispers ' I did not dare.'

'Peter blushes but does not speak. But when he hears Jesus asks Andrew 'Were you doing any wrong in coming? One must not dare do only evil things.' Peter intervenes: ' It was my fault...' he says frankly '...He wanted to bring me to you at once but I...I said...Yes, I said "I don't believe it" and I did not want to come. Oh! I feel better now!...'

Jesus smiles, and then says: 'And because of your sincerity, I tell you that I love you.'

'But I...I am not good...I am not capable of doing what you said in the synagogue. I am quick tempered and if anyone offends me eh! I am greedy and I like money...and in my fish business eh! Not always ...I have not always been honest. And I am ignorant. And I have little time to follow You to receive Your Light. What shall I do? I would like to become as You say...but...'
'It is not difficult, Simon. Are you acquainted a little with the Scriptures? Are you? Well, think of the prophet Micah. God wants from you what Micah said. He does not ask you to tear your heart apart, neither

does He ask you to sacrifice your most holy affections. He does not ask you for the time being. One day, without being requested by God, you will give God your own self.....But He will wait while the sun and the dew turn you, a thin blade of grass as you are now, into a sturdy, glorious palm tree. For now, He asks you only this: to be just, to love mercy, to take the greatest care in following your God. Strive to do that and Simon's past will be cancelled and you will become a new man, the friend of God and of His Christ. No longer Simon, but Cephas* the safe rock on which I lean.

'I like that! I understand that. The Law is so...is so...that is, I cannot comply with it any longer, as the rabbis have made it. But what You say, yes... I think I will be able to do it. And You will help me. ...Are You staying in this house? I know the owner.'

'I am staying here. But I am going to Jerusalem and after, I will preach throughout Palestine. I came for that. But I will often be here.'

'I will come, to hear You again. I want to be Your disciple...A little of the light will enter my head.'

'Your heart, above all, Simon...Your heart...And you, Andrew....have you nothing to say?'

'I am listening, Master.'

'My brother is shy.'

'He will become a lion. It is getting dark. May God bless you and grant you a good haul. Go now.'

'Peace be with you.'

And they depart.

'I wonder what He meant before when He said that I

will be fishing with other nets and catching different fish.' says Peter as soon as they're out.

'Why did you not ask Him?' You wanted to say so many things but you hardly spoke.'

'I ...was bashful. He is so different from all the other rabbis!'

'Now, He is going to Jerusalem...' Says John, with much longing and nostalgia. 'I wanted to ask Him if He would let me go with Him...But I did not dare...'

'Go and ask Him now my boy...' encourages Peter '...We left Him so... without a word of affection. Let Him at least know that we admire Him. I will tell your father.'

'Shall I go, James?'

'Go.'

John runs away... And he runs back overjoyed ' I said to Him: "Do You want me to come to Jerusalem with You?" He replied: "Come, My friend." ..Friend, He said! Tomorrow, I will be here at this time. Ah! To Jerusalem with Him!...'

* Cephas means Rock.

Jesus Meets Philip And Nathanael

John knocks on the door of the house where Jesus is
staying and is let in by a woman who then calls
Jesus.
They greet each other with a salutation of peace.
'You have come early, John'
'I have come to tell You that Peter asks You to pass by
Bethsaida. He has spoken to many people about
You...We did not go fishing last night. We prayed as
well as we could and we gave up profit...because the
Sabbath was not yet over. And this morning, we went
through the streets speaking about You...There are
many who would like to hear You...Will You come,
Master?'
'I will, though I must go to Nazareth before going to
Jerusalem'
'Peter will take You from Bethsaida to Tiberias in his
boat. It will be quicker for You'
'Let us go then.'
Jesus takes His mantle and knapsack but John
relieves Him of the knapsack. They say goodbye to the

Landlady and then set out from the village of
Capernaum on the shores of the Lake Galilee at
sunset, travelling by night to arrive at Bethsaida the
following morning.

When they arrive at Bethsaida, they find Peter,
Andrew, James and their wives waiting for them at
the entrance to the village.
'Peace be with you. Here I am.'
'We thank You, Master, also on behalf of those who
are waiting for You. It is not the Sabbath today but
will You speak Your words to those waiting to hear
You?'
'Yes, Peter, I will. In your house.'
'Come, then...' says Peter, overjoyed. '...This is My
wife and this is John's mother ...and these are their
friends. But there are other people waiting for You:
relations and friends of ours.'
'Tell them that I will speak to them this evening,
before I leave.'
'Master...please, stay one night at my house. The road
to Jerusalem is a long one, even if I shorten it by
taking You to Tiberias by boat. My house is poor, but
honest and friendly. Stay with us tonight.'
Jesus looks at Peter, and at all the rest waiting. He
looks at them inquisitively. Then, He smiles and says
'Yes, I will stay.'
Peter is delighted!
People look out from their doors and exchange
knowing glances with one another as the little party

walks through the village to Peter's house. A man calls James by name, speaks with him in a low voice, pointing to Jesus. James nods in assent and the man goes and speaks to other people standing at a crossroads.

They arrive at Peter's house and enter. There's a large smoky kitchen, with nets, ropes and fishing baskets in a corner, a long low fireplace- unlit- in the middle, two doors facing each other, one leading into the street, beyond which the rippling of the sky-blue lake is visible and the other into the kitchen garden where there's a fig tree and some vines, beyond which there's the dark low wall of another house.
'I offer You what I have Master, as best as I know how to...'
'You could not offer any more or any better because you are making your offering with love.'
'They give Jesus some water to refresh Himself, and then some bread and olives from which He takes a few mouthfuls to please them, thanks them and then eats no more.
Some inquisitive children look in from the kitchen garden and from the street and Peter frowns at the intruders to keep them out but Jesus smiles and says 'Leave them alone.'
'Master, do You want to rest? My room is here ...and Andrew's is over there. Take Your pick. We will not make any noise whilst You are resting.'
'Have you got a terrace?'
'Yes. And the vine, though it is still almost bare, gives

a little shade.'

'Then take me up there. I prefer to rest there. I will think and pray.'

'As You wish. Come.'

They go up a little staircase on the outside that rises from the kitchen garden up to the roof where there's a terrace surrounded by a low wall. There are no nets or ropes on the terrace but much bright light and...what a beautiful view of the blue lake!

Jesus sits down on a stool and leans back against the wall whilst Peter bustles with a sail, spreading it over the vine to provide shade from the sun. There's a breeze and silence and Jesus is visibly happy.

'I am going, Master.'

'Go. Go with John and tell people that I will be speaking here at sunset.'

But for two pairs of doves that come and go from their nests, and the twittering of sparrows, there is complete silence and Jesus remains alone and prays for a long time whilst the hours pass peacefully and quietly.

Then He gets up and walks round the terrace, looks at the lake, smiles at some children playing in the street and they smile back at Him. He looks further along the street at the little square about a hundred yards away from Peter's house then goes downstairs and looks into the kitchen ' Woman, I am going for a walk on the shore.'

Then He goes out and walks along the beach, near eleven children playing. 'What are you doing?' He asks them.

'We wanted to play at war. But he does not want to so we are playing at fishing.'

The boy who does not want to play at war is a bright faced, frail little fellow.

'He is right. War is a punishment of God to chastise men, and it is a sign that man is no longer a true son of God... When the Most High created the world, He made all things: the sun, the sea, the stars, the rivers, the plants, the animals but He did not make arms...He created man and gave him eyes that he might cast loving glances, a mouth to say loving words, ears to listen to such words, hands to give help and to caress, feet to run fast and assist our neighbours in need and a heart capable of loving...He gave man intelligence, speech, affections and taste...But He did not give man hatred. Why?...Because man, a creature of God, was to be love as God is Love. If man had remained a creature of God, he would have persevered in love and the human family would not have known either war or death.'

'But he does not want to make war because he always loses.'

'Jesus smiles. 'We must not reprove what is harmful to us simply because it is harmful to us. We must reprove a thing, when it is harmful to everybody...If a person says: "I do not want that because I would

lose", that person is selfish. Instead, the good child of God says: "Brothers, I know I would win but I say to you: let us not do that because you would suffer a loss". Oh! That fellow has understood the main precept! Who can tell Me which is the main precept?'
The eleven children say together ' You shall love your God with all your strength, and your neighbour as yourself.'
'Oh! You are clever children. Do you all go to school?'
'Yes, we do.'
'Who is the cleverest?'
'Him.' It is the frail little fellow who does not want war.
'What is your name?'
'Joel.'
'A great name! "...Let the weakling say: 'I am strong!" But strong in what? In the Law of the true God, to be amongst those who in the valley of Decision, He will judge to be His saints...But the judgement is already near. Not in the valley of Decision, but on the mountain of Redemption. There, the sun and the moon will grow dark with sorrow, the stars will tremble and shed tears of mercy, and the children of Light will be judged and separated from the children of Darkness. And the whole of Israel will know that its God has come. Happy those who would have recognised Him. Honey, milk and fresh water will descend into their hearts and thorns will become eternal roses...Which of you wants to be amongst those who will be judged saints of God?'
'I! I! I!'

'Will you love the Messiah then?'
'Yes! Yes! You! You! It's You we love. We know who
You are! Simon and James have told us, and our
mothers have told us. Take us with You!'
'Yes, I will take you if you are good. No more bad
words, no more arrogance, quarrels, no answering
back to your parents. Prayer, study, work, obedience.'
'And I will love You and come with You' and the
children all gather around Jesus in His blue garment
like a gay-coloured corolla around a long, deep-blue
pistil.
An elderly man approaches the group inquisitively
and when Jesus turns round to caress a child who is
pulling at His mantle, He sees the man and looks at
him with His intense probing gaze. The man blushes,
greets Him but then says nothing else.
'Come! Follow Me, Philip!' says Jesus, calling the
man by his name.
'Yes, Master.'
Jesus blesses the children and then walks back to
Peter's little kitchen garden and sits down with Philip.
'Do you want to be my disciple?'
'Yes, I do...but I dare not hope for so much.'
'I have called you.'
'Then I am Your disciple. Here I am.'
'Did you know about Me?'
'Andrew spoke to me about You. He said to me: "The
One you were pining for has come." Because Andrew
knew that I was yearning for the Messiah.'
'Your expectation has not been disappointed. He is in
front of you.'

'My Master and My God!'
'You are a well-intentioned Israelite. That is why I am manifesting Myself to you. Another friend of your is waiting, he, too, is a sincere Israelite. Go and say to him: "We have found Jesus of Nazareth, the son of Joseph, of the house of David, Him, of whom Moses and the prophets have spoken." Go.'
Jesus remains alone until Philip returns with Nathanael-Bartholomew.
'Here is a true Israelite in whom there is no deceit. Peace be with you, Nathanael.'
'How do You know me?'
' Before Philip came to call you, I saw you under the fig tree'
'Master, You are the Son of God. You are the King of Israel!'
'Because I said I saw you whilst you were meditating under the fig-tree, you believe? You will see greater things than that. I Solemnly tell you, that Heaven is open and because of your faith, you will see angels descending and ascending above the Son of man. That is, above Me, Who Am speaking to you.'

'Master, I am not worthy of such a favour!'
'Believe in Me, and you will be worthy of Heaven. Do

you believe?'
'I do, Master.'

Meanwhile, as evening approaches, a crowd gathers
on Peter's terrace and also in the kitchen.

Jesus speaks to them:

'Peace to men of goodwill...Peace and blessings to
their homes, their women, their children. May the
grace and the light of God reign in your homes and in
the hearts that dwell in them-

-You have wished to hear me. The Word is speaking.
It speaks with joy to the honest, with sorrow to the
dishonest, with delight to the holy and pure, with
mercy to sinners. It does not withhold itself, but has
come to spread out like a river that flows to irrigate
lands that need water, refreshing them and fertilising
them at the same time with humus.

- You want to know what is required to become
disciples of the Word of God, of the Messiah, Word of
the Father, Who has come to gather Israel together,
that it may hear once again the words of the holy and
immutable Decalogue and may be sanctified by them
and thus be purified for the hour of Redemption and
of the Kingdom, as far as man can be purified by
himself.

- Now, I say to the deaf, the blind, the dumb, the

lepers, the paralytic, the dead: "Rise, you are healed, rise, walk, may the rivers of light, of words, of sounds be opened for you, that you may see and hear Me and speak of Me."...But rather than to your bodies, I am speaking to your souls. Men of good will, come to Me without fear. If your souls are injured, I will cure them, if they are ill, I will heal them, if they are dead, I will raise them. All I want is your goodwill.

-Is what I ask for difficult? No. It is not. I do not impose on you the hundreds of precepts of the rabbis. I say to you: follow the Decalogue. The Law is one and immutable. Many centuries have gone by since it was given; beautiful, pure, fresh like a new-born creature, like a rose just opened on its stem. Simple, neat, easy to follow...But over the centuries, faults and trends have complicated it with many minor laws, burdens and restrictions and too many painful clauses......I bring you the Law, once again, as the Most High gave it and in your own interest, I ask you to accept it with sincere hearts, like the true Israelites of bygone times.

-You grumble, more in your hearts than with your lips, blaming the upper classes rather than humble people. I know. Deuteronomy states what is to be done; nothing else was necessary. But do not judge those who acted for other people, not for themselves. Do what God commands and above all, strive to be perfect in two main precepts: if you love God with all your souls, you will not sin because sin gives pain to God. Who loves does not want to give pain......

If you love your neighbours as you love yourselves, you will be respectful children to your parents, faithful husbands to your wives, honest merchants in your trade, without violence against your enemies, truthful in bearing witness, without envy of wealthy people, without incentive of lewdness for another man's wife...and as you do not wish to do to others what you do not wish others to do to you, you will not steal, or kill, or slander, or enter someone else's nest like cuckoos.

-Nay, I say to you: "Carry your obedience to the two precepts of love to perfection: love also your enemies.

-How much the Most High will love you since He loves man so much. Even though man became His enemy through original sin and because of his personal sins, He sent the Redeemer, the Lamb Who is His Son, that is I, Who am speaking to you, the Messiah promised to redeem you from all your sins, if you will learn to love as He does.

-Love. May your love become a ladder by which, like angels, you ascend to Heaven, as Jacob saw them, when you hear the Father say to each and everybody: "I will be your protector wherever you go, and I will bring you back to this place; to Heaven, the eternal Kingdom. Peace be with you."

The crowd utters words of emotional approval and slowly go away. Peter, Andrew, James, John, Philip and Bartholomew stay.

'Are you leaving tomorrow Master?'
'Tomorrow at dawn, if you do not mind.'
'I am sorry that You are going away but I do not mind
the hour; quite the contrary, it suits me.'
'Are you going fishing?'
'Yes, tonight, when the moon rises.'
'You did well, Simon, not fishing last night. The
Sabbath was not yet finished. Nehemiah* in his
reformation, wants the Sabbath to be respected in
Judah. Even today, too many people work on the
Sabbath: in presses, carry wood, wine and fruit, and
buy and sell fish and lambs. You have six days for
that. The Sabbath belongs to God. Only one thing you
may do on the Sabbath: you may do good to your
neighbour. But all profit must be excluded from such
help; **who infringes the Sabbath to make a profit
will be punished by God**...He makes a profit, He will
lose it during the other six days...He makes no profit?
He has fatigued his body to no avail because he did
not grant it the rest that Intelligence prescribed for it,
and thus, he irritated his soul having worked in vain,
and goes to the extent of cursing...The day of the Lord
is to be spent with your hearts united to God in sweet
prayer of love. You must be faithful in everything.'
* Nehemiah is the central figure in the book of
Nehemiah which describes his work in rebuilding
Jerusalem and purifying the Jewish community.
'But...Scribes and doctors, who are so severe with
us....do not work on Sabbath days, they do not even

give a piece of bread to their neighbours, to avoid the fatigue of handing it over but they practise usury** on the Sabbath. As it is not material work, is it legal to practise usury on a Sabbath?'

**The practise of lending money at unreasonably high rates of interest.

'No. Never. Neither on a Sabbath nor on any other day. Who practises usury is dishonest and cruel.'
'The Scribes and the Pharisees then...'
'Simon: do not judge. Do not do it.'
'But I have eyes to see...'
'Is evil only what you see, Simon?'
'No, Master.'
'Well then, why look at evil deeds?'
'You are right Master.'
'Well, tomorrow morning at dawn, I will leave with John.'
'Master...'
'Yes, Simon, what is it?'
'Master, are you going to Jerusalem?'
'You know I am.'
'I will also be going at Passover...so will Andrew and James.'
'Well? ...Do you mean that you would like to come with Me?... And your fishing?...And your profit?...You told me that you like to have money, and I will be away for many days; I am going to My Mother's first. And I will also go there on My way back; I will stop there to preach. How will you manage?'

107

Peter is perplexed, undecided...then he makes up his mind. 'I think...I will come. I prefer You to money!'
'I am coming, too.'
'And so Am I '
'We are going too, aren't we Philip? Asks Bartholomew.
'Come then, you will help me.'
'Oh! ...' exclaims Peter, even more excited at the idea of helping Jesus 'How shall we do that?'
' I will tell you. To do good, all you need to do is to do what I tell you. Who obeys always does good. We will now pray and then each of us will go and perform his duties.'
'What will you do Master?'
'I will continue to pray. I am the Light of the world but I am also the Son of man. Let us pray.... 'and Jesus recites the psalm that begins with 'Who rests in the help of the Most High, will live in the protection of the God of Heaven. He will say to the Lord: "You are my protector and my shelter. He is my God, I will hope in Him. He rescued me from the snares of fowlers and from harsh words ...."'

Judas Thaddeus At Bethsaida To Invite Jesus To The Wedding At Cana

Super is now over and Jesus, John, James, Peter and his wife are all sitting in Peter's kitchen talking and Jesus is taking an interest in fishing, when Andrews enters with news of visitors:
'Master, there is the man in whose house You are living, together with another man who says he is your cousin.'

Jesus gets up and goes towards the door ' Let them come in, He says. And when he sees Judas Thaddeus in the light issuing from the oil lamp and the fireplace, He exclaims 'You Judas?!'

'Yes, Jesus.' They kiss each other.
Judas Thaddeus is a virile handsome man in the
fullness of his manhood, tall, though not quite so tall
as Jesus, well-built and strong, of a dark brown

complexion like that of Joseph, the foster father of
Jesus, when he was young. His eyes are somewhat
similar to those of Jesus because they are a blue but
verge on Periwinkle, his brown beard is cut square
and his hair wavy is the same hue as his beard.

'I have come from Capernaum, I went there by boat
and I have come here by boat to gain time. Your
Mother sends me; She says: "Susanna is getting
married tomorrow, please come to the wedding." Mary
will be there, and also my mother and brothers...All
the relatives have been invited. You would be the only
one absent, and they ask you to come and make the
young couple happy.'

Jesus bows, slightly stretching out His arms and
says: A wish of My Mother's is a law for Me. But I will
come also for Susanna's and our relatives' sake.
Only...I am sorry for you...' and He looks at Peter and
the others. 'They are My friends...' He explains to His
cousin and then introduces them, beginning with
Peter and at the end, He says '...And this is John..'
with a special expression that makes Judas Thaddeus
look at John more carefully whilst the beloved disciple
blushes. Then, to His friends, He introduces Judas
Thaddeus saying:
'My friends, this is Judas, son of Alphaeus, My cousin
according to custom of the world because he is the
son of the brother of My Mother's spouse...A very
good friend of Mine, and a companion both in life and
work.'

'My house is open to you as it is to the Master. Sit down.' and then addressing Jesus, Peter asks ' So? Are we no longer going to Jerusalem with You?'
'Of course, you will come. I will go after the wedding feast. The only difference is that I will not stop at Nazareth any longer.'
'Quite right Jesus, because Your Mother is my guest for a few days...' says the man from Capernaum.
'...That is what we intend to do. She will also stay with me after the wedding.'
'This is what we will do. I will go in Judas's boat now, to Tiberias and from there to Cana. Then, with the same boat, I will come back to Capernaum with My Mother and with you...You will come the day after the next Sabbath, Simon...if you still wish to come... And we will go to Jerusalem for Passover.'
'Of course I want to come! Nay, I will come on the Sabbath to hear You in the synagogue.'
'Are You already teaching, Jesus?' asks Thaddeus.
'Yes, My cousin.'
'And you should hear His words!' Ah! No one else speaks like Him!'
Judas sighs. With his head resting on his hand, his elbow on his knee, he looks at Jesus and sighs. He seems anxious to speak but does not dare.
'What is the matter Judas?' says Jesus encouragingly. 'Why do you look at Me and sigh?'
'Nothing'
'No. It must be something. Am I no longer the Jesus of Whom you were fond?...From Whom you had no secrets?'

'Of course You are! And how I miss You, You the Master of Your older cousin...'

'Well then, speak.'

'I wanted to tell You...Jesus... be careful...You have a Mother...She has but You...You want to be a "rabbi" different from the others and You know, better than I do, that...that the powerful classes do not allow anything which may differ from the customary laws they have laid down. I know Your way of thinking...It is a holy one...but the world is not holy... and it oppresses saints...Jesus...You know the fate of Your cousin the Baptist...he is in jail, and if he is not yet dead, it is because that evil Tetrarch is afraid of the crowds and of the wrath of God. As evil and superstitious as he is cruel and lustful...You...what are You going to do? To what fate are You going to expose Yourself?'

'Judas, You are so familiar with My way of thinking, and that is what you ask Me?...Are you speaking on your own initiative? No, don't lie! You have been sent, certainly not by My Mother, to tell Me such things....'

Judas lowers his head and becomes silent.

'Speak, cousin.'

'My father... and Joseph and Simon with him...You know, for Your sake, because they are fond of You and Mary...do not look favourably on what You intend to do...and...they would like You to think of Your Mother...'

'And what do You think?'

'I...I...'

'You are drawn in opposite directions by the voices coming from High Above and those coming from the world. I am not saying from below...I say from the world. The same applies to James...even more so. But I tell you that above the world, there is Heaven...and above the interests of the world, there is the cause of God. You must change your ways of thinking. When you learn to do that, you will be perfect.'

'But... and Your Mother?'

'Judas, She is the only one who according to the way of thinking of the world, should be entitled to recall Me to My duty as a son: that is, to My duty to work for Her, and provide for Her material needs...to My duty to assist and comfort Her with My presence. But She does not ask for any of these things...Since She had Me, She knew She would lose Me, to find Me once again in a much wider manner than the small family circle...And since then, She has prepared Herself for that...
...Her unreserved voluntary donation of Herself to God is nothing new. Her mother offered Her to the Temple before She even smiled at life...And- as She told Me the countless times She spoke to Me of Her holy childhood, holding Me close to Her heart in the long winter evenings or in the clear starry summer nights-She gave Herself to God since the dawn of Her life in this world... And She gave Herself even more when She had Me, that She might be where I am,

fulfilling the Mission given to Me by God...Everybody will abandon Me at a certain moment, perhaps only for a few minutes, but everyone will be overcome by cowardice, and you will think that it would have been better, for your own safety, if you had never known Me...But She... Who understood and knows...She will always be with Me...

...And you will become Mine once again, through Her. With the power of Her unshaken, loving faith, She will draw you to Herself, and will thus bring you to Me, because I am in My Mother, and She is in Me, and We are in God...

...I would like you all to understand that, both you who are My relatives according to the world and you, friends and children in a supernatural way. Neither you nor anyone else knows Who My Mother is. But if you knew, you would not criticise Her in your hearts stating She is not capable of keeping Me subject to Her, but you would venerate Her as the closest friend of God, the Mighty Woman Who can obtain all graces from the heart of the Eternal Father and from Her beloved Son...I will certainly come to Cana. I want to make Her happy...

...You will understand better after the wedding.' Jesus is majestic and persuasive.

Judas gazes at Jesus, reflects, and then says ' And I will certainly come with You, with these friends, if You want me...because I feel that what You say is right. Forgive my blindness and my brothers'. You are so much holier than we are!'

'I bear no grudge against those who do not know
Me...I am also without ill feeling towards those who
hate Me...But I feel sorry for them because of the
harm they do themselves. What have you got in that
satchel?'
'The tunic Your Mother sent You. It is a big feast
tomorrow. She thinks that Her Jesus will need it so
that He may not look out of place amongst all the
guests. She worked from early morning till late night
every day, to have it ready for You. But She did not
finish the mantle; Its fringes are not yet ready and
She is very sorry about it.'

'It does not matter. I will wear this one, and I will
keep that one for Jerusalem. The Temple is much
more important than a wedding feast.'

'She will be so happy.'

'If you want to be on the way to Cana at dawn, you
ought to leave at once. The moon is rising and it will
be a pleasant crossing' says Peter.
'Let us go, then. Come, John. I am taking you with
Me. Goodbye, Simon Peter, James, Andrew. I will see
you on the eve of the Sabbath at Capernaum.
Goodbye, woman. Peace be with you and your house.'

Jesus goes out with Judas and John. Peter goes with
them as far as the lake and helps the, cast off.

116

END

If you enjoyed this book, please kindly submit a
review. Thank you!

Extracts from the Sequels

Where There Are Thorns, There Also Will Be Roses.

....

Jesus enters into the Temple complex accompanied
by His six disciples; Peter, Andrew, John, James,
Philip and Bartholomew, where there is already a
large crowd gathered inside as it is also outside the
Temple complex. In fact, looking down from the top of
the hill on which the Temple stands, the narrow
winding streets of Jerusalem are swarming with
pilgrims arriving in flocks from every part of town so
that the streets look like a moving multi-coloured
ribbon between its white houses and the whole town
is utterly transformed into a rare toy made of gaily
coloured ribbons converging towards the brilliant
domes of the House of the Lord.

But inside the complex, it is...a real market. The
serenity of the holy place has been destroyed by
people running, some calling, some contracting for
lambs, shouting and cursing because of the
extortionate prices, animals bleating as they are
driven into enclosures- rough partitions made of
ropes and pegs erected by merchants who stand at
the entrance to bargain with buyers.

There are blows with cudgels, bleatings, curses,

shouts, insults to servant boys who are not prompt in gathering or selecting the animals, abuses to buyers who haggle over prices or who turn away from a purchase and graver insults still to those who wisely brought their own lambs.

There is more bawling by the benches of the money changers where the legal exchange rate has been casually ignored and instead, without there being any fixed rate, the money changers now turned loan sharks, impose extortionate rates to hike up their profits just as they fancy and they do not joke in their transactions! The poorer the people are or the farther afield they come from, the more they are fleeced: the old more than the young and those from beyond Palestine even more than the old folk.

And it is clear that this is always the custom at least at Passover time; that the Temple becomes... a stock exchange or a black market.

A poor old man, one of many, looks gloomily again and again at the money he has saved in a whole year with much hard work. He takes it out and puts it back into his purse dozens and dozens of times, going from one money changer to another and sometimes in the end, returning to the first one, who then avenges himself for their original desertion by raising his commission. And the big coins pass regretfully from the clutches of its sighing owner into the grasping hands of the sharks who change them into smaller coins.

And then the poor old man moves on to another tragedy with the lamb merchants over the choice and payment for the Lambs. And if, as happens time and time again, the poor old man is also half blind then he is fobbed off with the most wretched looking little lamb.

An old couple- man and wife- bring back a poor little lamb, which has been rejected by those who perform the sacrifices as being faulty. The old couple cry and plead with the lamb merchant, who, far from being moved, replies in anger with crude words and cruder manners:
'Considering what you want to spend, Galileans, the lamb I gave you is even too good. Go away! Or if you want a better one, you must pay five more coins. '
'In the name of God! We are poor and old! Are you going to prevent us from celebrating this Passover, which may be our last one? Are you not satisfied with what you wanted for a poor little lamb? '
'Go away, you filthy lot. Joseph the Elder is now coming here. I enjoy his favour. God be with you, Joseph! Come and make your choice! '
Joseph the Elder, also known as Joseph of Arimathea, passes by, stately and proud, magnificently dressed, without as much as a glance at the poor old people weeping at the entrance to the enclosure. He enters the enclosure, picks a magnificent lamb and nearly bumps into the old couple as he goes out with his fat, bleating lamb.

Jesus who is now nearby, has also made His purchase, and Peter, who bargained for Him, is pulling a fairly good lamb. Peter would like to go at once where they offer the sacrifices but Jesus turns to the right, towards the dismayed, weeping, undecided old couple, who are knocked about by the crowds and insulted by the vendor.

Jesus, Who is so tall that the heads of the poor old souls reach only up to His heart, lays one hand on the shoulder of the woman and asks her: ' Why are you crying, woman? '

The little old woman turns round and she sees the young, tall, stately man, in a beautiful new white tunic and a matching snow-white mantle. She mistakes Him for a doctor because of His garments and His aspect and her surprise is the greater because doctors and priests neither pay attention to the poor nor do they protect them from the stinginess of merchants. She explains to Jesus the reason for their tears.

'Change this lamb for these believers. It is not worthy of the altar, neither is it fair that you should take advantage of two poor old people, only because they are weak and unprotected. ' says Jesus to the lamb vendor.

'And who are You? '

'A just man. '

'By Your way of speaking and Your companions', I know You are a Galilean. Can there be a just man in Galilee? '

'Do what I told you, and be a just man yourself. '
'Listen! Listen to the Galilean Who is defending His
equals! And He wants to teach us of the Temple! ' The
man laughs and jeers, imitating the Galilean accent,
which is more musical and softer than the Judaean.
Many people draw nearer to them and other
merchants and moneychangers take the side of their
fellow merchant against Jesus.
Amongst the people present there are two or three
ironical rabbis. One of them asks: 'Are You a doctor?
', in a manner that would try even the patience of Job.
'Yes, I am.'
'What do You teach? '
'This I teach: to make the House of God a house of
prayer and not a usury or a market place. That is
what I teach. '
Jesus is formidable. He looks like the archangel on
the threshold of Eden and even without a flashing
sword in His hand, the beams from His eyes strike
the impious mockers like lightning. Jesus has
nothing in His hands. All He has is His wrath. And
full of wrath, He walks fast and solemnly between the
money changers' benches: He scatters the coins that
have been so meticulously sorted according to their
values, He overturns the benches and tables throwing
everything onto the ground with great clattering
noises. Amidst the clanging of rebounding metals and
beaten wood, angry cries, shrieks of terror and shouts
of approval rise mingled. But Jesus is not quite
finished yet.

He snatches some ropes used to hold oxen, sheep and lambs from the hands of the stable boys and uses them to make a very hard lash with the slip knots that are real scourges. Then He lifts the lash and swings it striking mercilessly with it.

Yes...mercilessly.

The unforeseen storm hits heads and backs. The believers move to one side admiring the scene; the guilty ones, chased as far as the external wall, take to their heels, leaving their money on the ground and abandoning their animals in a great confusion of legs, horns and wings, some of which, startled, run and fly away. The bellows of oxen, bleatings of sheep and fluttering of turtle doves and pigeons, add to the bursts of laughter and the shouting of the believers as they mock the escaping credit sharks drown even the plaintive chorus of lambs being slaughtered in another yard.

Priests, rabbis and Pharisees rush to the spot. Jesus is still in the middle of the yard, turning from the chase, the lash still in His hands.

'Who are You? How dare You do that, upsetting the prescribed ceremonies? From which school are You? We do not know You, neither do we know where You come from.'

'I am He Who is Mighty. I can do anything. Destroy this true Temple and I will raise it to give praise to God. I am not upsetting the holiness of the House of God or of the ceremonies, but you upset it by allowing His House to become the centre of credit sharks and merchants. My school is the school of God. The same school the whole of Israel had when the Eternal God spoke to Moses. You do not know Me? You will know Me. You do not know where I come from? You will learn.'

Then ignoring the priests, Jesus turns to the people, standing tall in His white tunic, with His mantle open and blowing in the wind behind His back, His arms outstretched like an orator reinforcing the key point of his speech, He says: ' Listen, Israel! In Deuteronomy it is said: "You are to appoint judges and scribes at all the gates... and they must administer an impartial judgment to the people. You must be impartial; you must take no bribes, for a bribe blinds wise men's eyes and jeopardizes the cause of the just. Strict justice must be your ideal, so that you may live in rightful possession of the land that Yahweh your God is giving you." '

'Listen, Israel. In Deuteronomy it is said: "The priests and scribes and the whole of the tribe of Levi shall have no share or inheritance with Israel, because they must live on the foods offered to Yahweh and on His dues; they shall have no inheritance among their brothers, because Yahweh will be their inheritance."'

'Listen, Israel. In Deuteronomy it is said: "You must not lend on interest to your brother, whether the lack be of money or food or anything else. You may demand interest on a loan of a foreigner; you will lend without interest to your brother whatever he needs." The Lord said that. But now you see that in Israel judgments are administered without justice for the poor. They are not inclined to justice, but they are partial with the rich, and to be poor, to be of the common people means to be oppressed. How can the people say: "Our judges are just" when they see that only the mighty ones are respected and satisfied, whereas the poor have no one who will listen to them? How can the people respect the Lord, when they see that the Lord is not respected by those who should respect Him more than everyone else? Does he who infringes the Lord's commandment respect Him? Why then do the priests in Israel possess property and accept bribes from tax- collectors and sinners, who make them offerings to obtain their favours, while they accept gifts to fill their coffers? God is the inheritance of His priests. He, the Father of Israel, is more than a Father to them and provides them with food, as it is just. But not more than what is just. He did not promise money and possessions to His servants of the sanctuary. In eternal life, they will possess Heaven for their justice, as Moses, Elijah, Jacob and Abraham will, but in this world they must have but a linen garment and a diadem of incorruptible gold: purity and charity, and their bodies must be subject to their souls, which are to be subject to the true God, and their bodies are not to be masters over their souls and against God.

I have been asked on what authority I do this. And on what authority do they violate God's command and allow in the shade of the sacred walls usury on their brothers of Israel, who have come to obey the divine command? I have been asked from what school I come and I replied: "From God's school" Yes, Israel, I have come from and I will take you back to that holy and immutable school.

Who wants to know the Light, the Truth, the Way, who wants to hear once again the voice of God speaking to his people, let him come to Me. You followed Moses through the deserts, Israel. Follow Me, because I shall lead you through a far worse desert, to the true blessed Land. At God's command, I will draw you to it, across an open sea. I will cure you of all evils lifting up My Sign.

The time of Grace has come. The Prophets expected it and died waiting for it. The Prophets prophesied it and died in that hope. The just have dreamt of it and died comforted by that dream. It is now here. Come. "The Lord is about to judge His people and have mercy on His servants," as He promised through Moses. '

The people crowding round Jesus stand open-mouthed listening to Him. Then they comment on the new Rabbi's words and question His companions. Jesus goes to another yard, separated from the first one only by a porch and His friends follow Him.